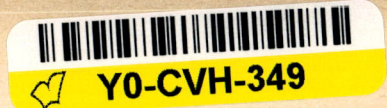

THE ECONOMICS OF PERSONAL INJURY

ERRATA

Contents: in Figures 7.3 to 7.6 " min. £600 " should read " max. £600 ".

Page 117: the title of the figure should be: " Figure 7.3, Amount of settlement (max. £600)".

Pages 118, 119, 120: the titles of the respective figures should read: " max. £600 " for " min. £600 ".

The economics of personal injury

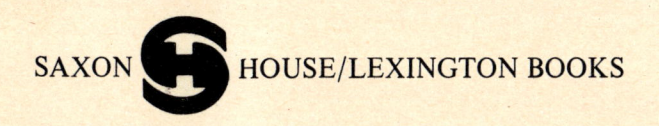

DEBAPRIYA GHOSH

DENNIS LEES

WILLIAM SEAL

University of Nottingham

SAXON HOUSE/LEXINGTON BOOKS

© Copyright Debapriya Ghosh, Dennis Lees and William Seal, 1976

All rights reserved. No part of this publication may be reproduced, stored in a retrieval system, or transmitted in any form or by any means, electronic, mechanical, photocopying, recording, or otherwise without the prior permission of D.C. Heath Ltd.

Published by

SAXON HOUSE, D.C. Heath Ltd.
Westmead, Farnborough, Hants., England.

Jointly with

LEXINGTON BOOKS, D.C. Heath & Co.
Lexington, Mass. USA.

ISBN 0 347 0111 X
Library of Congress Catalog Card Number 75−28611
Printed in Great Britain by Robert MacLehose and Company Limited
Printers to the University of Glasgow

Contents

Acknowledgements	viii
1 Introduction	1
2 Some aspects of accident research	5
A taxonomy of accident research	5
The application of accident research	6
3 An aggregative analysis of road accidents	15
Introduction	15
The model	17
Results of the model for all roads in Great Britain	22
Results of the model for motorways in Great Britain	28
4 Towards a social policy	39
Introduction	39
Policy objectives	39
An economic theory of accident occurence and prevention	56
Conclusion	63
5 Optimal speed on the motorway and some shadow prices	67
Introduction	67
Optimal speed: the theoretical background	67
The model	68
The valuation problem	76
An application of the model	78
Some shadow prices	82
6 Other accident areas	87
Accident classification	87
Product liability	89
Industrial accidents	93
Statistical information	95
Some economic works on industrial accidents	97

7	The economics of compensation	101
	Accidental injury as a social problem	101
	The costs of compensation systems: some empirical evidence	113
	Conclusion	124
8	Conclusions	127
	Bibliography	129
	Index	135

List of Tables

2.1	Road and light conditions in fatal accidents (England and Wales)	9
2.2	Potential savings in deaths and serious injuries from increased seat belt use	13
3.1	Some measures for total casualties	23
3.2	Some measures for slight injuries	23
3.3	Some measures for serious injuries	24
3.4	Some measures for fatalities	24
3.5	Motorway casualties: log-linear regression equations without intercepts: January 1970 to December 1971	32
3.6	Motorway casualties: log-linear regression equations without intercepts: January 1972 to March 1974	32
3.7	Measures of neutrality of technical innovation from the previous two tables	33
3.8	Motorway casualties: linear equations for January 1972 to March 1974	34
3.9	Motorway casualties: log-linear equations for January 1972 to March 1974	34
3.10	Hypothetical savings of lives and limbs on the motorways: October 1973 to March 1974	35
4.1	The rankings of classified industries according to accident rates (p) and weekly earnings (α), 1969–72	62
5.1	Changes in the optimal speed due to an increase in petrol price	75
5.2	Optimal average speeds (m.p.h.)	81
5.3	Valuations of time	83
5.4	Valuations of petrol	84
7.1	Ratio of administrative costs to compensation	114

| 7.2 | Correlation coefficients for the Common Law Compensation Group, £0–600 | 122 |
| 7.3 | Correlation coefficients for the Common Law Compensation Group, £601–£8,200 | 122 |

List of figures

2.1	Hourly injury accident rate at New Year 1964–65 (Great Britain)	8
2.2	Trends in numbers of car involvements in fatal and serious accidents 1963–72	11
2.3	Level of seat belt wearing amongst front seat occupants of cars and light vans with seat belts fitted 1972–73	12
3.1	Technical change in preventing road accidents	18
3.2	Shifts of α for slight and total injuries	26
3.3	Shifts of α for fatal and serious injuries	27
4.1	Bargaining solutions to accident externality	45
4.2	Bargaining possibilities in public good	47
5.1	Optimal speed	68
5.2	Change in the optimal speed	72
5.3	Change in optimal speed due to a rise in petrol price	74
5.4	Speed and fuel consumption	80
7.1	The impact of moral hazard on insurance premiums	105
7.2	Effect of accidental injury to B on A's equilibrium wealth transfer	108
7.3	Amount of settlement (Min. £600)	117
7.4	Loss of earnings (Min. £600)	118
7.5	Duration of illness (Min. £600)	119
7.6	Wait (days) (Min. £600)	120

Acknowledgments

We have had invaluable help from a great many people and a wide variety of institutions. On road accident research we have obtained much useful advice and data from Mr R.F.F. Newby of the Transport and Road Research Laboratory; from Dr C.C. Wright of University College London; and Dr L.W. Ackroyd and Mrs S. Trench of our Civil Engineering and Planning Departments respectively at Nottingham. We have had useful discussions with Dr J.P. Bull of the Medical Research Council at Birmingham Accident Hospital, with Jenny Phillips of the Centre for Socio-Legal Studies at Oxford, and with several people at the Department of Environment, Meteorological Office, University of Birmingham Accident Research Unit, Accident Investigation Unit of the Nottinghamshire County Council and Child Accident Research Unit, Department of Psychology here at Nottingham. Valuable comments, criticisms and help on the earlier drafts of our work have come from Professor A. Prest, Mr C.S.M. Sutcliffe, Mr M. Ricketts, Mr N. Doherty, Mr B. Chiplin, Mr M. Nair, Mr M.H. Atkins, Ms B.A. Lawson and many others. But we alone are responsible for any errors that may remain in the final product. Finally we gratefully acknowledge the financial assistance from the Social Science Research Council for our continuing project on the economics of personal injury.

Debapriya Ghosh
Dennis Lees
William Seal
Department of Industrial
Economics, University of
Nottingham
August, 1975

1 Introduction

This book is about accidents to persons, their causes, consequences and the way in which they are compensated. It is not about personal injuries arising from intentional criminal acts. Neither is it concerned with the long and short term disablement arising from sickness and disease. The problem of defining the scope of our book in this manner is that it immediately embroils us in the controversy concerning the definition of an accident.

It will be seen, however, that such a problem is not a major concern of our book. As social scientists, our interest in personal injury does not extend to the technical or legal definitions of what constitutes accidental injury as opposed to sickness although, as may be seen in chapters 4, 6 and 7, we cannot entirely evade these difficult issues. But for the most part we shall let the definition grow out of an examination of the problem.

The scheme of the book is to present a method of accident research and policy formulation. This method is firmly based on economic rationale and techniques. It seeks to bring together in a coherent and, hopefully, enlightening way disparate ideas and materials. While basically economic in outlook, it draws on medicine, engineering, law, social administration and insurance.

Our main aim is to present a method or approach to accident research. We do not suggest that our book comprehensively reviews all aspects of the accident phenomenon. For example, it is evident that the bulk of our original empirical work on accident *causation* has been conducted on road accidents. We do feel, however, that our approach is sufficiently general to be applied to social policy formulation over the whole gamut of personal injury problems. Thus our theoretical and empirical work on *compensation* encompasses all possible causes of personal injury, irrespective of location.

We are involved in an area with a wide diversity of disciplines. It is probable that, to many people, the relevance of economics in the field of accident research is not at all obvious. Indeed, the traditional economic preoccupations with the exchange and production of goods, employment, wealth and international trade may seem far removed from the problem of personal injury. It is therefore understandable if the exact nature of the contribution that economics can make is at first sight rather obscure.

We feel that the layman usually views the scope of economics too narrowly. Economics is a science which studies the logic of individual and social choice. It is not merely concerned with the consumption and production of material goods. Certainly, choices have to be made on how many guns are to be made and how much butter. However, a society also needs to decide on how many accidents to permit and how many resources should be used to try to prevent them. These are the questions we ask and propose answers to in this book. More mundanely, accidents use up people and material goods. Since prevention also consumes scarce resources, we are faced with the familiar classic economic problem even though it is applied in a relatively unfamiliar area.

We feel, however, that we have contributed a little more than this general choice-orientated approach. We have applied an economic concept, the aggregate production function together with the techniques of econometrics, in order to estimate the contribution of various factors leading to road accident causation. This part of the book must be seen as a direct contribution to the technical analysis of accidents. It seems clear to us that the technical relationships must be established before the choice problem can be presented. For example, we needed to establish that more speed resulted in more accidents before we could specify the speed—accident trade off model in chapter 5.

Until very recently, the field of accident policy has been largely unexplored by economists with the best known contributions coming from lawyers and engineers (see for example, G. Calabresi[1] and R.J. Smeed[2]). The situation is rapidly changing as more and more articles on accidents and compensation appear in the economics literature. We have cited many of the most recent contributions in what is rapidly becoming a major area of economic research. Our particular emphasis is on positive rather than normative analysis. Furthermore, we have chosen a level of aggregation which may not appeal to some academic economists but has given us in our own opinion a comparative advantage in terms of practical explanations and solutions.

In chapter 2 we briefly review the possible methods of conducting accident research. We also introduce the complexities involved in interpreting and using the resulting accident data. It is intended that the case study material should illustrate the sort of problems that we deal with on a more systematic basis in chapters 3, 4 and 5.

In chapter 3 we propose a method by which some pattern may be derived from the mass of available statistical data. We introduce the concept of the shifting aggregate production function. We apply our model both to identify long term accident trends on British roads and, particularly, in order to estimate the short term effect of speed and traffic volume on accident level.

In the next chapter we change tack slightly by reviewing the ethical and methodological basis of economics and considering how it may be used to evolve a social policy for accident control. After briefly considering the externality argument we adopt a more aggregative approach and by specifying a social welfare function are able to derive the formal requirements for an optimal accident policy.

In chapter 5 we combine the technical relationships between speed and rate of petrol consumption and also between accidents, speed and traffic volume estimated in chapter 3 with our normative economic analysis of chapter 4 in a cost-benefit analysis of average motorway speed. In particular we propose a model from which the optimal speed can be calculated given any set of the valuations and prices chosen. In the second half of the chapter we use this model in order to estimate some shadow prices of life and time by assuming the actual average speed observed in our empirical period to be the optimal speed.

In chapter 6 we briefly consider the problem of accident classification. We review the literature on product liability and finally consider the particular problems posed by industrial accidents.

The emphasis in earlier chapters is on accident causation and optimal accident levels. In chapter 7 we approach the problem of compensation of accident victims as an end in itself rather than as a by-product of the accident level optimisation process. In particular we consider the difficulty of using micro-economic theory in order either to explain or suggest reforms of existing institutional arrangements for compensation. We present some empirical work we have conducted on the transaction costs of the various compensation systems and on their effectiveness in compensating victims in a particular industry.

In chapter 8 we summarise our results and suggest further possible lines of research.

Notes

1 G. Calabresi, *The Costs of Accidents,* Yale University Press, New Haven, 1970.

2 R.J. Smeed, 'Some statistical aspects of road safety research', *Journal of the Royal Statistical Society,* Series A 112, p. 1–23, 1949; R.J. Smeed, 'The usefulness of formulae in traffic engineering and road safety', *Accident Analysis and Prevention,* vol. 4, 1972.

2 Some aspects of accident research

2.1 A taxonomy of accident research

While it would be difficult and presumptuous of us to attempt to survey and evaluate the whole field of accident research, it may help the reader to locate our own position if we review some of the alternative methods of accident research. Although any distinctions are to some extent rather arbitrary, we suggest that accident research falls into five main categories. These are:

1. Laboratory tests.
2. Semi-controlled experiments.
3. Case study method.
4. The epidemiological approach.
5. Statistical model building.

1 *Laboratory tests*

This approach lends itself most easily to tests on non-human subjects. For example, experiments to test the optimal design of motorway crash barriers or asbestos suits may be carried out under carefully controlled conditions. The method is less useful in the testing of drugs where although the level of technical skill of the experimenter may be very high, he is inevitably limited in his ability to use the human subjects for whom the drug may be designed.

2 *Semi-controlled experiments*

This approach is very common in road accident research. The experimental conditions can only be controlled to some extent. For example, it may be possible to compare the accident results for a length of motorway with full lighting with a similar stretch with no lighting but it is inevitable that results will be distorted by extraneous factors such as changes in traffic volume and the vagaries of the weather. It may be difficult to identify a firm relationship between cause and effect. For example, if the accident rate falls for a period on the stretch of road where the speed limit is being more rigorously enforced for experimental reasons, is it because of the resulting lower speeds, or is it because driver behaviour is improved by the increased police presence?[1]

3 Case study method

As we shall see in later chapters, accident information is often generated largely by analysing past disasters. In many situations, such as with a toxic drug, it may be extremely difficult to know how many tests to carry out before it can be released for human use. The complex effects of the drug may only emerge after a number of years of experiments as was the tragic case with thalidomide.

4 The epidemiological approach

As its name suggests, this approach was first applied to analyse the possible causes of epidemics. An outbreak of a disease was related to a number of factors concerning the age, sex and location of the host in an attempt to identify one or more common factors which may have contributed to the epidemic. In chapter 6, we suggest that the NEISS system[2] may be regarded as a sophisticated form of epidemiological accident research.

5 Statistical model building

The difference between this approach and the epidemiological approach is that it generally employs more sophisticated statistical techniques in order to describe and analyse the same sort of data. for example, Smeed[3] has fitted a mathematical function to international road accident data. In our own work, we have begun with a specific model which we test with British road accident data. There is a distinction between the Smeed approach and our own method. We will elaborate on this in chapter 3.

2.2 The application of accident research

Since a large portion of this book is devoted to explaining how accident research may be applied in a social policy for accident prevention, we will confine ourselves to presenting three examples of applied accident research which illustrate, in a non-rigorous manner, the basic interaction between accident research and policy formulation — an interaction which we will develop more formally in subsequent chapters. Our examples illustrate the typical pattern of (a) the introduction of an exogenous change into the accident generating environment; (b) a statistical analysis of the effects of the change combined with an attempt to discount the effects of other extraneous factors; and (c) an evaluation of the social costs and benefits of a policy change.

Our first example is drawn from a study made in England and Wales during the Christmas and New Year period of 1964–65. The purpose of the study[4] was to evaluate the results of '... the national "drink and driving" campaign, which was held in November and December 1964'. The problem for the Road Research Laboratory was to find out the effect of the campaign '... after allowing for the effects of wet weather, the day of the week on which Christmas Day fell and any tendency for the casualty rate to change systematically over a period of years ...' The laboratory came up with the tentative conclusion that the campaign resulted in 10 to 15 per cent less casualties than expected. Our main interest here in the Report lies in the hourly injury accident rate per million motor vehicle-miles and we reproduce the graph in Figure 2.1. The graph shows that the injury rate in dark periods has been always higher than during the daytime. Or to put it differently, darkness seems to be a significant factor in increasing the accident rate. Of course, people usually drink in the evenings and the high rate of accidents before the breath-tests came into operation in September 1967 could be due to the effect of excessive drinking and not lack of light alone. If the introduction of breath-tests has a significant preventive effect on the accident rate, darkness would be expected to have less influence than before.

From the same Report let us now look at the possible contribution made by wet and icy roads to fatal accidents.

Table 2.1 does not refer to volume of traffic and it contains only fatalities, so it cannot be inferred from the above evidence if wet weather or lack of light have any significant contribution in causing road casualties. But it does suggest that those two factors may be important in influencing the rate of road casualties.

It was suggested from the Road Research Laboratory's investigations during Christmas 1959 and 1963 that alcohol might contribute significantly to the increase of fatality ratios and on the basis of such knowledge the Ministry of Transport spent £479,000 on the drinking and driving campaign from 18 November 1964. This campaign has been tentatively credited with reducing the casualty rates to some extent. If this claim was true, the social valuation of the casualties saved during the period (and also in subsequent periods when the campaign was discontinued, but its effect lingered on, possibly with declining impact) must exceed £479,000 to justify that accident preventive expenditure. It might have been thought so by the authorities, because the 1967 Road Safety Act introduced a limit on drinking before driving (80

Figure 2.1
Hourly injury accident rate at New Year 1964–65 (Great Britain)

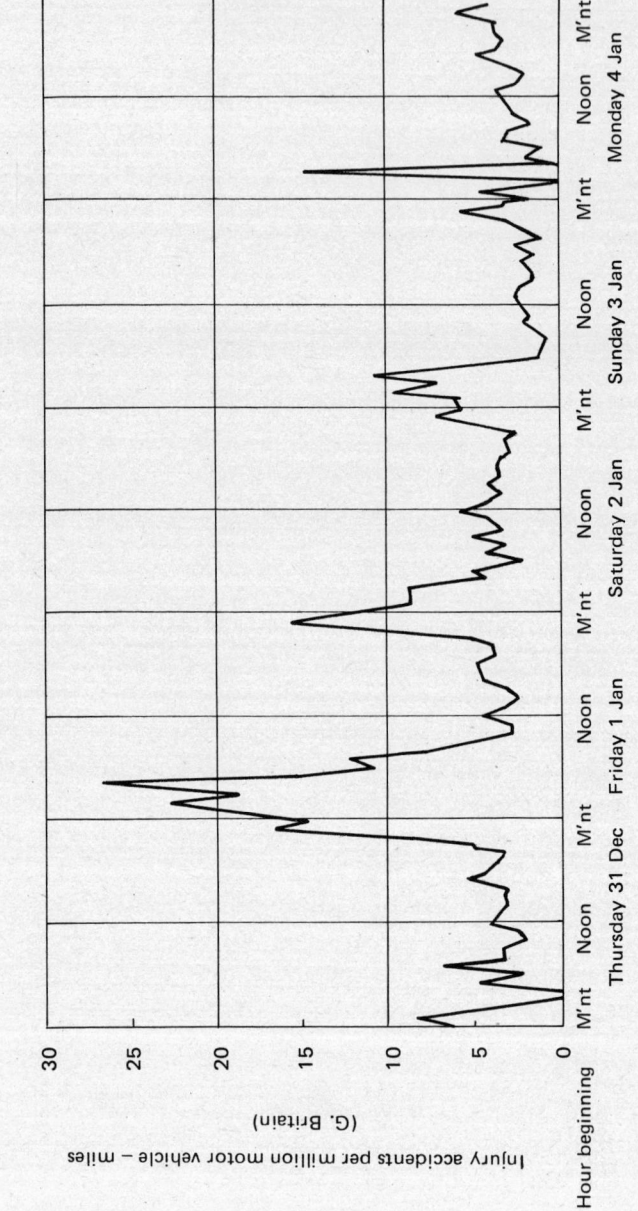

Table 2.1

Road and light conditions in fatal accidents (England and Wales)

Date	Light hours Dry	Wet	Icy	Dark hours Dry	Wet	Icy	Total
23 December 1969	5	1	—	12	4	1 (1)	23 (1)
24 December 1969	9 (1)	2	—	11 (2)	15 (2)	1 (1)	38 (6)
25 December 1969	6	—	1	4	5	—	16
26 December 1969	4	—	—	2	2	3	11
27 December 1969	1	—	2	1	2	4	10
28 December 1969	1	2	4	2	1	2	12
6 days	26 (1)	5	7	32 (2)	29 (2)	11 (2)	110 (7)

*Numbers in brackets (included in the main figure) refer to accidents when fog or mist was present.

Source: 'Road Accidents in December 1964 and January 1965', *Road Research Technical Paper*, no. 79, HMSO, 1965, p. 6.

milligrams/100 millilitres blood alcohol levels) which must have had some effect on the casualty rates on roads, as evidenced by Figure 2.2.[5]

This trend in the relevant casualty rate shows that the 1967 Road Safety Act and its implementation have been reducing the casualties on British roads. This law might also have reduced the benefit to some people from their drinking above the limit and driving afterwards. Added to that are the labour and capital cost to the police force to implement the Act. If these totals have been less than the casualties and damage saved, the introduction of the law and its implementation costs from year to year may be regarded as a move for the better.

A similar point may be made about the introduction of the seventy miles per hour speed limit trial on all roads in Great Britain not already subject to a lower limit. Before a final decision was made on this speed limit, it was investigated by the Road Research Laboratory[6] which found that in 1966, after a year's restriction on speed, there was '... a marked reduction in the number of cars travelling at high speeds'. On accidents, '...there were some 480 fewer fatalities and casualties on motorways as a whole...', though injury accidents '...on all-purpose main roads subject to the 70 m.p.h. speed limit were about 3½ times fewer than would have been expected without the limit ...' The Report did not make any conclusive comment on the economic gain of the process. To do that, they needed to evaluate the extra journey time that the speed limit incurred, the implementation cost of the speed limit, the petrol saved and the depreciation of cars and tyres delayed due to lower speed and of course the social valuation of personal injuries and damage to cars and other non-human capital items. Whatever the context, drinking and driving, speeding, the use of seat belts, etc., there is a broad policy dilemma for the authorities. They may restrict behaviour by imposing some law and expending resources to implement the law, like speed limits to reduce accidents. Alternatively, they may try to persuade the potential victims to abide by some norm like drinking up to a specified limit before driving or wearing a seat belt before every journey. The ultimate policy to be undertaken should not only have its potential benefits outweighing its potential costs but also its net gain should be more than is obtainable from other policy alternatives. Let us illustrate the argument with the help of our first example; the case of wearing seat belts.

From July 1972, the authorities in Great Britain allotted some resources to advertise the case for the wearing of seatbelts. They first[7] started with the Yorkshire and Lancashire Television Areas. This was then extended to London and ultimately to the rest of the country. National surveys carried out in this period registered an increase in the rate of seat belt wearing. Later on, however, when less resources were expended in this publicity campaign the rate declined from its earlier high level during the peak of the campaign. This demonstrates the well-known theorem in the literature [8] of advertising that there are 'cumulative or lagged effects of advertising [which] may be defined as: (i) the effect of a perceived advertisement which influences two or more successive purchasing decisions of a consumer with regard to a given product ... or (ii) the effect of an advertisement which influences consumer buying behaviour beyond the period of its appearance' (Report). These lagged effects diminish in their impact with time when the rate of publicity is not kept up to its original level. The government statistical service provides us with a graph[9] which illustrates the above theorem in our example of seat belt wearing and we reproduce that below in Figure 2.3.

The graphs in Figure 2.3 show that when publicity was at its peak the response was high, but with declining and ultimately very little or no advertisement effort the intended effect on seat belt wearing also dropped. Some of the benefits of a high level of seat belt use were also estimated. We reproduce the results in Table 2.2.

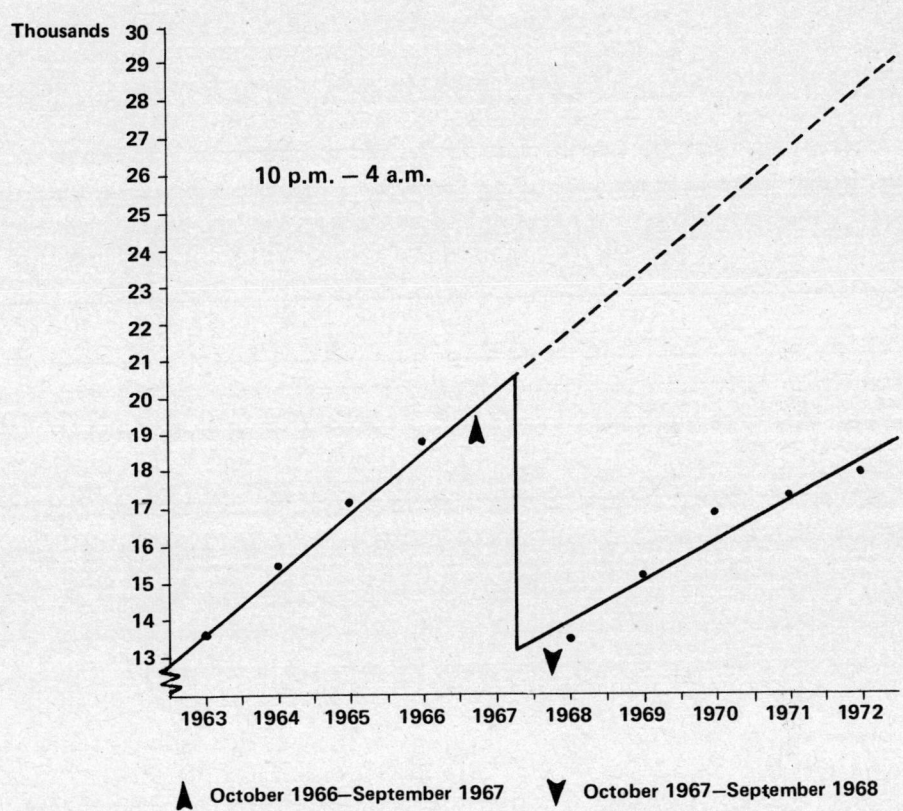

Figure 2.2
Trends in numbers of car involvements in
fatal and serious accidents 1963–72

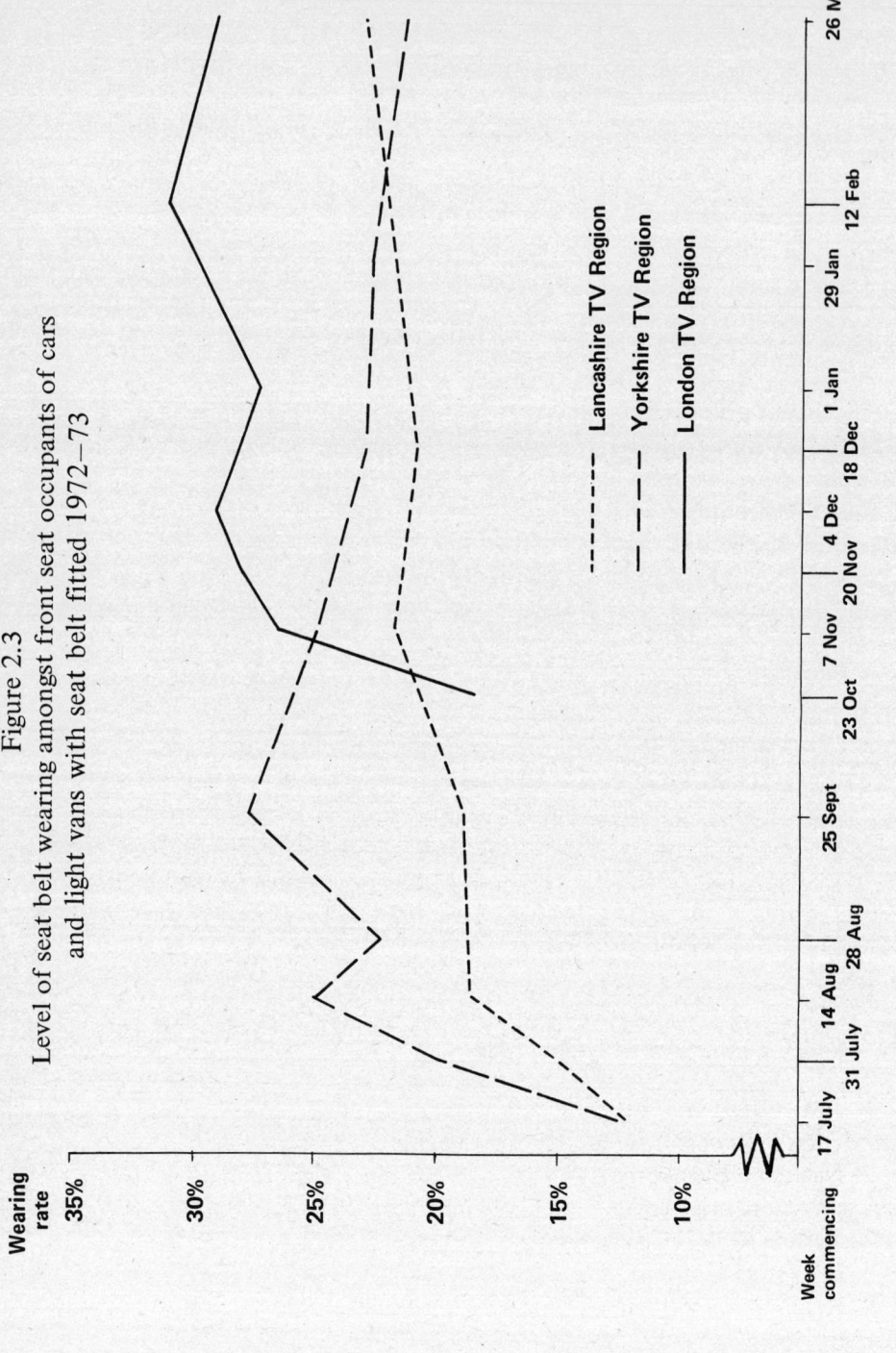

Figure 2.3
Level of seat belt wearing amongst front seat occupants of cars and light vans with seat belt fitted 1972–73

Table 2.2

Potential savings in deaths and serious injuries from increased seat belt use

Year	70% wearing rate	100% wearing rate
1969	4,500	7,500
1970	6,000	9,500
1971	7,000	11,000
1972	8,000	13,000

Source: *Road Accidents in Great Britain, 1972,* p. xiii, HMSO.

To this list of potential benefits from the increased use of seat belts we can add the savings in the thousands of minor injuries avoided in the same process. Now, the question is what would be the optimal way of realising a target percentage wearing rate. A continuous process of publicity may be tried until the required rate of seat belt wearing is achieved and resources would have to be expended subsequently to stabilise that rate. Alternatively a law may be passed to make the wearing of seat belts compulsory, as in Australia, New Zealand, certain areas in France, Czechoslovakia and other European countries. Here we may note that the implementation of this law affects the costs of enforcing it. Whichever of these two alternatives leads to a higher rate of return in terms of net potential benefit per pound of resources expended would be the better policy. It may be added here that in the case of drinking and driving, for example, the implementation of law may require more capital equipment compared to implementing legal compulsion on seat belt wearing. But the labour input in the latter case is likely to be much higher than the first case, since the whole population of mobile cars would be the subject of scrutiny.

Notes

1 J.M. Munden, 'An experiment in enforcing the 30 mile/hour speed limit', *RRL Report LR 24,* Harmondsworth 1966.

2 National Electronic Surveillance System. This is an accident monitoring system designed for the US Consumer Product Safety Commission (see chapter 6).

3 R.J. Smeed, op.cit.

4 Road Research Laboratory, 'Road Accidents in December 1964 and January 1965', *Road Research Technical Paper,* no. 79, HMSO, 1965.

5 *Road Accidents in Great Britain,* 1972, 1973, HMSO.

6 Road Research Laboratory, 'Report on the 70 m.p.h. Speed Limit Trial', *RRL Special Report,* no. 6, HMSO, 1967.

7 *Road Accidents in Great Britain,* 1972, 1973, HMSO.

8 One such study, where these phenomena are discussed may be found in K.S. Palda, *The Measurement of Cumulative Advertising Effects,* Prentice-Hall 1972.

9 *Road Accidents in Great Britain,* 1972, p. xii.

3 An aggregative analysis of road accidents

3.1 Introduction

In this chapter we present the concept of an accident as an event 'produced' by a multitude of factors, some of which are controllable by society and others generally beyond control. This may be described by a functional form, known in economic jargon as a 'production function'. We may visualise this function to be shifting over time due to all sorts of technological changes and resource allocations in preventing accidents. When we apply this model to the British data we may note the increasing effectiveness of all the long and short term preventive measures in the form of a gradual decline in the magnitude of the apparently non-controllable factors like the volume of traffic and weather in explaining the frequency of road casualties.

The causes of road accidents, however, and the personal injuries and deaths from such accidents are numerous and varied. These causes have been broadly classified in various investigations of the nature of road accidents and the classification usually depends on the particular factor of interest for the problem at hand. For example, after the seventy m.p.h. speed limit came into operation in this country on 22 December 1965, the Road Research Laboratory investigated (RRL 1967) the effect of this speed limit on the frequency of accidents. Another exhaustive study from the same source (RRL 1965) analysed the effect of the consumption of alcohol by the drivers on 'accidents and behaviour', during December 1964 and January 1965. While knowledge of such marginal impacts of certain factors are useful for cost-benefit analysis of some policy measures, they are rather difficult to identify. Volume of traffic, speed of travel, traffic density, road designs, car designs, physical and mental state of the drivers and the pedestrians, weather, policing of traffic and other laws all contribute to the aggregate casualties on our roads. Since all these factors operate simultaneously, it is almost impossssible to conduct an experiment by changing one set of causes while retaining all others at any given and unchanging level to determine the particular marginal impact of the changing factor on road accidents.

Some mathematical and/or statistical methods may, however, be adopted to identify the effect of a group of factors. These approaches have already been used in economics and in other social sciences and we now investigate how far they may help our understanding of the present problem. While these techniques have their limitations, at the present state of the availability of information and of the method of accident research at an aggregate level, they do seem to have some marginal advantage of their own.

A well-established relation in the analysis of accidents has been worked out by R.J. Smeed since 1949. His equation[1] relating fatalities in road accidents to population and the number of motor vehicles in a country fits the accident records of many countries for a wide period from 1905 to 1970 (Smeed 1972, fig. 1). To quote Smeed (1972):

> ... the chance of a vehicle being involved in an accident involving another vehicle would increase with the number of other vehicles since there are more possibilities of collision when traffic increases. The fact that the formula shows that in practice the number of deaths per registered motor vehicle decreases instead of increasing as motorization increases suggests that there are major counterbalancing factors.

Smeed suggests three main items for the 'counterbalancing factors':

1 A changeover from motorcycles, which are highly accident prone, to cars as the popular passenger transport would decrease the fatality rate.
2 With the increase in motor vehicles people would learn to cope with them better than they used to.
3 When the accident rate is regarded as much too high there is a social demand to do something to reduce it and '... something is in fact done'. (Smeed 1949)

There have been some objections to the concept of broad aggregate relations in accident analysis by A. Peranio[2] who emphasises the lack of accuracy in formulae involving human beings as opposed to those involving inanimate objects and asks for a prior conceptualisation of '... the process involved in order to identify the major variables that have a measurable effect on what is being considered'. But, one might argue, the quantitative measures in all the social sciences, which are much less accurate than those in natural sciences, are nonetheless useful and an attempt to find some order in the frequency of accidents in this vein could conceivably contribute to our knowledge in this field. Peranio's emphasis, however, on the need for a prior scheme of causal relationships is, no doubt, important and we would follow his methodology in presenting our model in the next section '... to establish a reasonable functional relationship that links the major variables' (Peranio, 1971).

In our own approach we assume that road accidents are caused by some factors which are within control, and others beyond control. The effect of the factors which are generally beyond a direct control, like volume of traffic, or factors which are beyond any sort of control, like weather, would give us some indication of the effectiveness of all short term and long term preventive measures to reduce road accidents. If we could put them all together and call them the 'technological factor' in reducing accidents, we might be able to identify the declining influence of non-controllable factors on road accidents and even get an index of the effectiveness of preventive measures of all kinds. This procedure of looking into the aggregate road accidents might be put to use for social policy on accident prevention if one could estimate the total periodical costs from personal injuries and damages to cars and to other non-human capitals in such cases and also identify the flows of capital expenditure and other costs in all possible preventive measures.

3.2 The model

We develop a model outlining the above features of road accidents along the lines of an article by R.M. Solow.[3] Solow differentiated between the increases in output per unit of labour input caused by an increased use of capital and also by a technical change in the production process. Our analogy to Solow's theory, as hinted above, distinguishes between the influence of some apparently non-controllable factors on casualties from those of all other factors assumed to be controllable. Let us write it in a functional form as follows:

$$X = F(V, W, t) \tag{3.1}$$

where X = number of casualties,
V = miles of motoring,
W = weather index and
t = time.

In time t we include all other (mainly controllable) factors influencing casualties, e.g. driving under the influence of alcohol, stringent MOT tests, time spent by the police force on traffic duties, road designs, traffic designs, motor manufacturing designs, speed limits, driving tests, insurance etc. These factors are changing all the time and we may visualise the net impact of them for a certain level of V and W during a period of time on X. One would expect that this net impact, *ceteris paribus,* of A (all other controllable factors) at time t would be to reduce the effect of V and W on X, because of the continuing technical innovation of all sorts in the prevention of accidents. If this continuing technical innovation may be supposed to be neutral in its effect on V and W in affecting X, we may write equation (3.1) as follows:

$$X = A(t) \cdot f(V, W) \qquad (3.2)$$

where $A(t)$ 'measures the cumulated effect of shifts over time' (Solow, 1957). Let us illustrate the relation with the help of a diagram.

Figure 3.1
Technical change in preventing road accidents

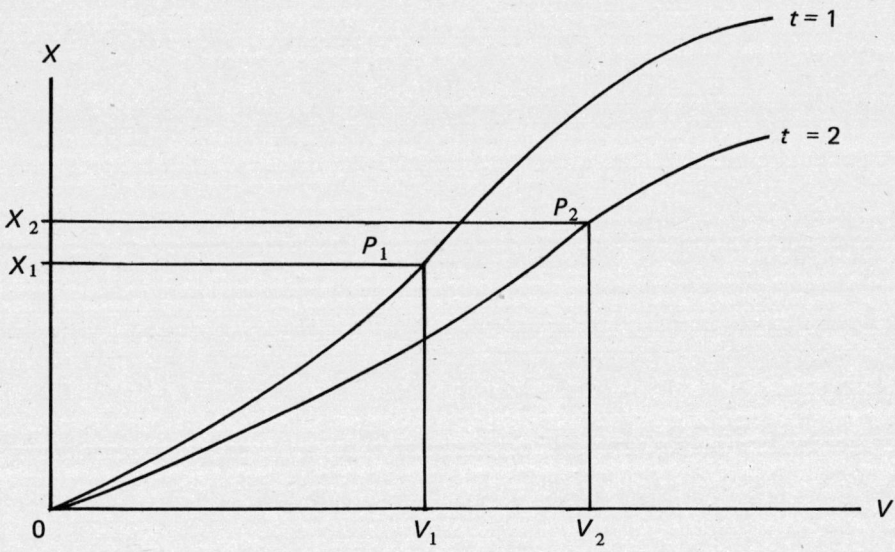

In Figure 3.1, for two consecutive time periods, say two years, we observe the magnitudes of casualty and of volume of traffic. Let us assume weather to remain more or less similar in those two years to illustrate our hypothesis, though in the subsequent formulation of our theory both volume of traffic and weather indices are allowed to vary simultaneously. Now, the rise in the casualty figures could be partially due to a rise in the volume of traffic from period 1 to period 2 as shown in the points P_1 and P_2 in Figure 3.1. But during this period the impact of volume of traffic on casualty might have diminished owing to technical innovation and also to resource allocation in preventing accidents. This is depicted by a downward shift of the curve relating X to V for a certain level of W. Again, along a curve for any particular time period one would expect some learning process on the part of drivers and pedestrians, so that casualties would rise less than proportionately with a rise in V. If we now go back to equation (3.2) above, we may look into the effect of simultaneous changes in V and W and can derive the following relation:

$$\frac{\dot{X}}{X} = \frac{\dot{A}}{A} + A \cdot \frac{\delta f}{\delta V} \cdot \frac{\dot{V}}{X} + A \cdot \frac{\delta f}{\delta W} \cdot \frac{\dot{W}}{X} \qquad (3.3)$$

$$= \frac{\dot{A}}{A} + \frac{\delta X}{\delta T} \cdot \frac{\dot{T}}{X} + \frac{\delta X}{\delta W} \cdot \frac{\dot{W}}{X} \qquad (3.4)$$

$$= \frac{\dot{A}}{A} + S_V \cdot \frac{\dot{V}}{V} + S_W \cdot \frac{\dot{W}}{W} \qquad (3.5)$$

where variables with dots on them imply time derivatives, and

$$\frac{\delta X}{\delta V} = A \cdot \frac{\delta f}{\delta V} \; ; \frac{\delta X}{\delta W} = A \frac{\delta f}{\delta W} \; ; \; S_V = \frac{\delta X}{\delta V} \cdot \frac{V}{X} \; ; \; S_W = \frac{\delta X}{\delta W} \cdot \frac{W}{X}$$

But this form of Solow's model (i.e. equation 3.4) may not be applied here, because we do not have information on the elasticity of casualties with respect to weather (S_W) or to volume of traffic (S_V) for each time period. This information is needed if we have to disentangle $\dot{A}/A$, or the cumulative effect of technical changes in preventing accidents from equation (3.5). We may, however, use equation (3.4) to use available information to calculate $\dot{A}/A$. This could be achieved from the estimation of $\delta X/\delta V$ and $\delta X/\delta W$ through a multiple regression of X on V and indices for W for the initial time period from which we start our investigation. The number of observations for such a regression should be so selected that it would not contain within itself a known big change in A or it may not be so numerous as to suggest that A changed considerably during the said period of observation. But before we discuss the estimation procedures let us go back to equation (3.2) above and look into certain implications of this formulation.

It should be noted that items included in $A(t)$ in equation (3.2) may affect both the volume of V and the elasticity of X with respect to V, whereas only the elasticity magnitude is affected for W due to any change in A during a period of time t. The recent experience of high petrol price and the subsequent speed limit would be a case in point. The high costs of petrol would cause a voluntary reduction in driving by motorists, affecting V in our model whereas a limit on speed may affect both V and the elasticity of X with respect to V. Thus the variable V in our model may not be exactly non-controllable and policy may be designed to reduce V to achieve other objectives like enforcing a lower consumption of petrol, whereupon the subsequent fall in road casualties comes out only as a desirable by-product. But so long as the combination of all possible policy and technical changes leaves the marginal rate of substitution between V and W unaffected throughout the different shifts of the assumed road casualty relation in nature, we can write equation (3.1) in the form of equation (3.2).

Another point on $A(t)$ may be noted here. Some technical improvements are designed specifically to reduce the personal injury element of road accidents, whereas others are meant for reducing the frequency of road accidents themselves. We are, however, interested in the final impact of all preventive measures on personal injury from road accidents and not in the damages to cars or other non-human costs of these events.

We applied equation (3.4) to the British data for all classified roads, starting from 1964 and using monthly information on the relevant variables. The difficulty lies here in finding a proper index or indices for weather which contains all the important elements of it which have turned out to be significant in influencing accident frequency in several investigations. But, whatever index or indices one may choose for W here, some monthly changes are so large that the estimate of A/A is unduly affected by this $\dot{W}$. This forced us to abandon equation (3.4) as a method to find out $A(t)$ and led us to develop an ad hoc estimation procedure for the magnitudes we are interested in.

The method we finally adopted to measure the changing pattern of the influence of apparently non-controllable factors on the frequency of casualties may be described as follows. We may divide the period 1964 to 1973 in five separate two-year periods or ten separate (i.e. non-overlapping) one-year periods and assume that $A(t)$ would not change much during any of the periods under observation. Fortunately for our purpose, the seventy m.p.h. speed limit and the restrictions on driving under the influence of alcohol both came towards the end of 1965 and 1967 respectively, allowing us to make this classification. Next we write equation (3.2) above in the Cobb-Douglas form with two indices for W. Studies in this country (RRL 1965, 1967,) and West Germany[4] suggest that wet roads and driving in darkness are specially accident prone. There are other elements of weather like fog which must be responsible in influencing the frequency of accidents. But lack of time series data on some indices of those other elements forces us to use monthly rainfall and daily averages of monthly sunshine data as proxy variables for wet roads and darkness or time of day affecting the frequency of road accidents. Let us now write the tested relation as follows:

$$X = A. V.^{\alpha} W_1^{\beta_1} W_2^{\beta_2} \qquad (3.6)$$

where, X = number of road casualties of a particular type in one month;
V = million vehicle miles in one month;
W_1 = millimetres of rainfall in one month; and
W_2 = hours of mean daily sunshine in a month.

If we now rewrite equation (3.6) in log form we have:

$$\log X = \log A + \alpha \log V + \beta_1 \log W_1 + \beta_2 \log W_2 \qquad (3.7)$$

This is the equation we go on to estimate. In terms of the ideas developed above we expect all the elasticity magnitudes — α, β_1 and β_2 to be less than unity, α and β_1 to be positive and β_2 to be negative. We also expect each of α, β_1 and β_2 to follow a declining trend as we proceed from the early (1964–65) to the later estimates of the model.

It may be mentioned here that though rainfall and sunshine do not normally coincide, millimeters of rainfall in a month and hours of average daily sunshine for a month do not necessarily have a high negative correlation. In fact, this correlation coefficient for our five time periods was −·16, −·28, −·24, −·42 and −·25. The correlation between volume of traffic and hours of sunshine, however, is likely to be high since driving is more popular during the summer months than in the winter period. This correlation for our five time periods was ·83, ·80, ·69, ·70 and ·83. This high correlation between the two independent variables in equation (3.7) indicates the chance of multi collinearity causing inefficient estimates of either α or β_2, or of both. Again, the specification of our model in terms of twenty-four serial monthly casualty data is likely to cause autocorrelation, implying underestimates of the variances for the regression coefficients. In our interpretation of the results for equation (3.7), using four different types of casualty data, we should, therefore, look into these problems of autocorrelation and multicollinearity to determine whether our elasticity figures are reliable.

Finally, a value for the continuous technical progress in the prevention of accidents may not be measured from the intercept term in equation (3.7) in the same sense as one could get it from $A(t)$ in equation (3.2) above. But some indication of the effectiveness of technical progress may be visualised from the other estimates, so long as they are unbiased and efficient. If there is any technical progress in preventing road accidents we could expect the explanatory power of the model in equation (3.7) to diminish with time and also the elasticity of road casualties with respect to the non-controllable factors V, W_1 and W_2 to follow a diminishing trend in absolute values as one progresses in time.

3.3 Results of the model for all roads in Great Britain

We present the results of our estimation in Tables 3.1 to 3.4. Road casualties are classified in three different groups according to the published data on them. This classification itself is a matter of dispute. There is a wide variation of the severity of injury in each group of casualties and even the numbers of fatalities caused by road accidents may be more or less than the published data on them. Serious injuries are defined as all cases of 'in-patient' treatments in a hospital for road casualties but they may range from minor injuries to cases bordering on fatalities. Many slight injuries may not be recorded at all if they are not reported to the police. Thus, there is some doubt in the magnitude of X in our model above from the published sources. J.P. Bull and B.J. Roberts analysed[5] a sample of 1200 patients at the Birmingham Accident Hospital and found many discrepancies '... in the police records on which official statistics are based'. But if we could assume that such 'errors in variables' are not too large and the distribution of the severity of injuries in one group follows some 'normal' type distribution to make the classification meaningful, we may still use the published data on personal injuries from road accidents. This process may, however, be erroneous if the used data are distributed about a false mean. This may be the case of slight injuries where underestimation could be systematic.[6] These limitations of the published casualty data should be kept in mind in our use of them in the tables below.

The volume of traffic data are based on the Road Research Laboratory monthly estimates of millions of miles of motoring on the classified roads. The recent available data at the time of our work on all roads for the five years, 1969, 1970, 1971, 1972 and 1973, are not used because data on classified roads only are available for the earlier years and we need to make all the years comparable. Weather statistics for the whole of Great Britain are calculated from the England, Wales and Scotland figures for the same with a weight[7] of 4 to 1.

Table 3.1
Some measures for total casualties

Periods	Parameters	α	β_1	β_2	$\frac{\alpha}{\beta_1}$	$\frac{\alpha}{\beta_2}$	$\frac{\beta_1}{\beta_2}$	R^2	D.W.
1	1964–65	·680	·111	–	6.126	–	–	·814	·864
2	1966–67	·684	·103	–	6·641	–	–	·672	1·317
3	1968–69	·744	–	–·091	–	–8·176	–	·651	1·293
4	1970–71	·564	–	–·077	–	–7·325	–	·506	1·284
5	1972–73	·502	·111	–·088	4·523	–5·705	–1·261	·563	1·700

Table 3.2
Some measures for slight injuries

Periods	Parameters	α	β_1	β_2	$\frac{\alpha}{\beta_1}$	$\frac{\alpha}{\beta_2}$	$\frac{\beta_1}{\beta_2}$	R^2	D.W.
1	1964–65	·706	·110	–	6·418	–	–	·842	·877
2	1966–67	·659	·106	–	6·217	–	–	·685	1·339
3	1968–69	·723	–	–·078	–	–9·269	–	·639	1·357
4	1970–71	·528	–	–·067	–	–7·881	–	·496	1.238
5	1972–73	·496	·109	–·080	4·550	–6·200	–1·363	·564	1·745

Table 3.3
Some measures for serious injuries

Periods		α	β_1	β_2	$\dfrac{\alpha}{\beta_1}$	$\dfrac{\alpha}{\beta_2}$	$\dfrac{\beta_1}{\beta_2}$	R^2	$D.W.$
1	1964–65	·611	·113	—	5·407	—	—	·731	·946
2	1966–67	·750	·093	—	8·065	—	—	·654	1·226
3	1968–69	·782	—	−·116	—	−6·741	—	·681	1·197
4	1970–71	·576	—	—	—	—	—	·308	1·762
5	1972–73	·516	·116	−·101	4·480	−5·109	−1·149	·555	1·669

Table 3.4
Some measures for fatalities

Periods		α	β_1	β_2	$\dfrac{\alpha}{\beta_1}$	$\dfrac{\alpha}{\beta_2}$	$\dfrac{\beta_1}{\beta_2}$	R^2	$D.W.$
1	1964–65	—	·131	−·178	—	—	−0·736	·468	1·250
2	1966–67	·725	—	−·215	—	−3·372	—	·457	1·691
3	1968–69	·979	—	−·239	—	−4·096	—	·558	1·347
4	1970–71	·841	—	−·210	—	−4·005	—	·598	1·848
5	1972–73	·553	—	−·198	—	−2·793	—	·528	1·549

The results for the estimation of equation (3.7) are presented in Tables 3.1 to 3.4. It may be pointed out at the outset that the existence of autocorrelation at the 1 per cent level of the $D.W.$ test statistic is indicated only for the first time period in Table 3.1 and the lack of it for the last time period in all four tables and also for the fourth period in Table 3.3 and the second and fourth periods in Table 3.4. For the rest of the models the test is inconclusive. Again it has been already noted that we can rewrite equation (3.1) in the form of equation (3.2), if technical change leaves the marginal rate of substitution unaffected. In our case this measure is $\frac{T}{W} \cdot \frac{\beta}{\alpha}$ and we have to note if it remains constant during the five time periods for each model. This we can measure at any particular value for $\frac{T}{W}$. At this value we have to check if $\frac{\beta}{\alpha}$ is changing drastically over time. If it does, our assumption of neutrality of technical change may not be justified. If it does not change much, we may be allowed to rewrite equation (3.1) in the form of equation (3.2) and estimate our *a priori* relations between different types of casualties and the apparently non-controllable factors causing them. We therefore presented measures of the ratios $\frac{\alpha}{\beta_1}, \frac{\alpha}{\beta_2}$ and $\frac{\beta_1}{\beta_2}$ in the four tables above whenever both the coefficients in a ratio are statistically significant at 95 per cent level. The three coefficients in each model are also presented only under similar circumstances. Let us now look into each table separately.

In Table 3.1, we first look into total casualties. The sign pattern here is according to expectation, though four out of fifteen coefficients under scrutiny are not significantly different from zero. The values of R^2 follow a declining trend suggesting a similar pattern of influence of these apparently non-controllable factors on total road casualties. The influence of wet roads (β_1) remains constant at an elasticity, just over 10 per cent, while the influence of darkness registers a similar value between 8 to 10 per cent. The elasticity of total casualties with respect to volume of traffic exhibits a declining trend, thus confirming our hypothesis that technical improvement and increased resource allocation in preventing accidents could be revealed in the gradual fall in the probability of being involved in an accident for the same amount of driving. The fact that α does not show a steady decline may be explained by the existence of some lag. There is continuous adjustment by the drivers and the pedestrians to the new preventive measures and there may be some lag in their effectiveness. On one such measure of speed limits during pre-war and post-war years in the UK and other countries for the urban and rural areas, the experience [8] shows that, '... the full effect of these measures was felt over a period of time and it is unlikely that they were responsible for the instant fall in accidents which followed in the months after the introduction of the urban speed limit, though in the longer term they produced a considerable and lasting improvement.' We present below the changes in the values of the elasticity of different types of casualties with respect to the volume of traffic. They illustrate the process of continuous adjustment around a declining long term trend. We may note here that all the elasticity values are less than unity, suggesting some learning process in coping with the apparently non-controllable factors which cause accidents. This element of learning process is an important factor in explaining the negative slope of R.J. Smeed's (1949, 1972) formula for fatalities and it is confirmed in our four tables above.

Figure 3.2

Shifts of α for slight and total injuries

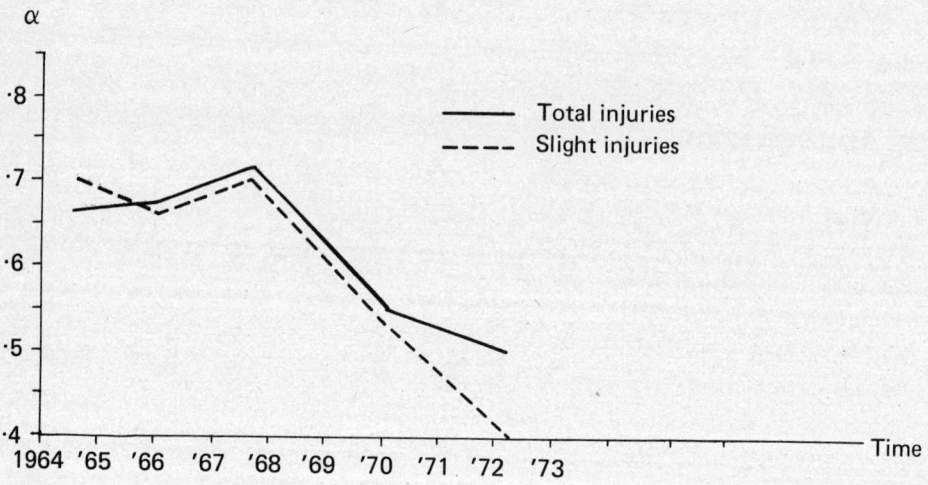

We note that the ratios of the coefficients $\frac{\alpha}{\beta_1}$ and $\frac{\alpha}{\beta_2}$ are not exactly constant over time. The lowest values of the two ratios are about 70 per cent of the corresponding highest values. Though they do not indicate strict neutrality of technical change, we may, perhaps, be allowed to assume from this sample that the marginal rate of substitution between V and W_1 and V and W_2 remains more or less constant over the decade under study.

Figure 3.3
Shifts of α for fatal and serious injuries

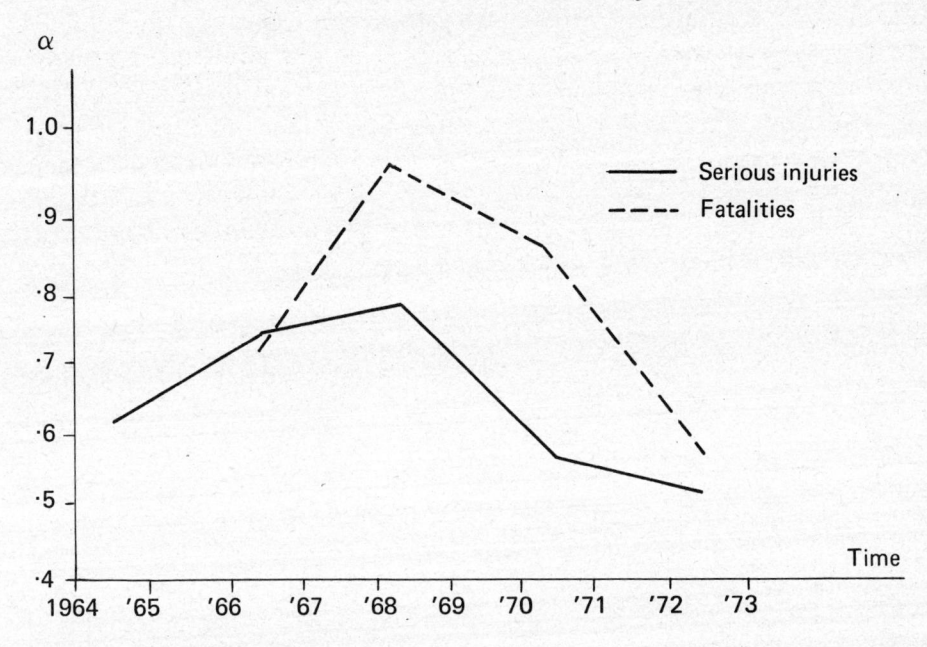

Most of the comments made about total casualties apply to slight injuries in Table 3.2. This is so, because the major proportion of total casualties are slight injuries and what we observe for the latter is closely repeated when we sum up the two other types with slight injuries. There are, however, some differences in Table 3.3 from the two earlier tables. Values of R^2 do not decline steadily here and the fourth value of β_2 turns out to be insignificant at 95 per cent level. Otherwise, the sign-pattern is also according to expectations here and all the elasticities turn out to be less than unity. The values of β_1 here are not much different from its values in the earlier tables. The values of β_2 for serious injuries are, however, appreciably higher than the corresponding values for slight injuries. It may be repeated here that all the parameters with a significance level of less than 95 per cent are ignored here. In our earlier work[9] we included some of them and the interpretation of results was slightly different from the present one when we dismiss them all as not being significantly different from zero. It may be mentioned here that the existence of multicollinearity between V and W_2 and between W_1 and W_2 in affecting casualties seems to have reduced the sample variance of the estimates of β_1 and β_2 in all the tables. This would, therefore, imply our inability to estimate those marginal impacts, rather than those effects

27

being equal to zero.

Let us now look into fatalities in Tables 3.4. All the elasticities here are less than unity, the sign-pattern is as expected and β_2, for the first time, comes out to be significant at 95 per cent level in all the time periods. We have already looked into the variation of α in Fig. 3.2. above. β_1 is significant only for the first time period and it is rather high compared to other types of injuries. β_2 is somewhat constant around $-\cdot 2$ and the values of R^2 do not suggest a declining trend as may be the case in the other two types of injuries. Taken as a whole, the results suggest that in the cases of slight and serious injuries technical progress and resource allocation to prevent accidents have mainly contributed to the gradual decline of apparently non-controllable factors affecting road casualties whereas in the case of fatalities it is not so clear. Values of β_1 and β_2 for slight and serious injuries seem to have stabilised and there may be some room for improvement for both these values for fatalities. Apart from their use as a fresh interpretation of casualty records, these estimates may provide one with a useful measure of the success of preventive methods over time for a country and may also be used for comparing such methods among different countries. They may also be used as targets for social policy on accident prevention. For example, a low value of α like $\cdot 2$ or $\cdot 3$ for a particular type of injury may require enormous marginal effort which may not turn out to be optimal for the community. Again, β_1 (i.e. the rate of influence of wet roads on casualties) for fatalities in Table 3.4 may be considered to be sufficiently low and efforts may now be channelled towards reducing β_2 (i.e. the rate of influence of darkness on road casualties) in this case. In other words, the influence of wet roads on fatalities from the road accidents may be temporarily regarded as tolerable and efforts should better be made to reduce the influence of darkness or bad light on them.

3.4 Results of the model for motorways in Great Britain [10]

We have already seen in the previous section that while road accidents and casualties are generally regarded as primarily random events, in their aggregate they may exhibit some order. For example, road casualties during a certain period in a region or a country are likely to be related to the total volume and typical density of traffic, the weather conditions and the average vehicle speed and its dispersion on the roads. There are many other causes behind the frequency of casualties. It may be possible to distinguish between different groups of causes and to analyse the effects of one group on this frequency, as we have already done above. In this section we are conducting another such experiment with the recent casualties data from the British motorways. Given that motorways are homogenous in many technical characteristics, we hope to be able to find some order in the way traffic volume (corrected for density), weather and average vehicle speed influence the frequency of casualties. Again, since one of our main interests here is the influence of speed on casualties, we choose motorways where the speed limits are generally uniform.

Casual empirical observation suggests that dangerous situations frequently arise on motorways when vehicles in different lanes are travelling at markedly different average speeds. It could be argued that the use of a single average speed figure will disguise this potential source of accidents. There is some evidence, however, that when the speed limit is lowered we can expect this difference in average vehicles speeds to diminish. Similarly, the introduction of a minimum speed limit will also cause a reduction in the variance of traffic speed. It could be argued that the use of a single average traffic speed will subsume the possible relationship between accidents and variations in vehicle speeds if the speed limit is lowered as dramatically as it was over the period of our observations. Clearly, an interesting extension of our model would be to include a variable for *variance* of traffic speeds. Unfortunately we found that the data available to us was insufficiently detailed to include the necessary information on variance. We hope, however, that our average speed variable has to a large extent captured the effect of the change in variance.

In the earlier section we have used the concept of a shifting 'production function' for road casualties to analyse the effect of some apparently uncontrollable factors. We present the following hypothesis in similar form as follows:

Let $$X = F(t, V, W, S) \tag{3.8}$$

be the relevant production function, where

X = number of casualties,
V = volume of traffic,
W = weather index,
S = average vehicle speed,
and t = time.

This function is expected to be shifting in a favourable trend (i.e. for more effective accident prevention) due to all sorts of technical innovation, law and resource allocation designed to reduce the frequency of casualties. If the total effect of all such measures leave the 'marginal rate of substitution' between V, W and S unaffected, one might rewrite equation (3.8) as follows:

$$X = A(t) \cdot f(V, W, S) \qquad (3.9)$$

where $A(t)$ 'measures the cumulated effect of shifts over time' (Solow, op. cit.).

The functional forms used for the above relation are linear and log-linear, as follows:

$$X = A \cdot V^\alpha \cdot S^\beta \cdot W^\gamma \qquad (3.10)$$

and

$$X = A + aV + bS + cW \qquad (3.11)$$

where X = number of motorway casualties of a particular type during a month;
V = million vehicle miles per month per available motorway mile;
S = average motorway speed for a month;
W = weather index— hours of daily average sunshine in a month;
and the exponents α β and γ are the relevant elasticities and a, b and c are the relevant coefficients.

The reasons for expecting S to affect X on *a priori* grounds have been well documented[11] in the studies on road accidents and we do not go into that here. We apply this model to two periods: (i) January 1970 to December 1971 and (ii) January 1972 to March 1974. We expect the parameters to be estimated (viz., α, β and γ) for the two periods to be similar and we do not expect them to indicate any trend as we have done in our earlier application of the model above. But there are some problems even to this comparison.

The available measures[12] of average vehicle speed on the motorways indicate very small variation until winter 1973–74 when the petrol crisis forced the government to reduce the speed limit to fifty m.p.h. The subsequent reinstating of the seventy m.p.h. limit has enabled us to observe some sharp variation in average speed which was almost completely absent before. This lack of variation in our first time period presents us with the problem of multicollinearity with respect to average speed and the intercept term. Average speed being more or less stable throughout this first period of our experiment we can not get proper estimates for both β and b in this model. Thus a manageable comparison of the two time periods would involve the use of a regression model which leaves out the intercept term. This would restrict the explanatory power of the models since we would not be able to consider the other important variables described earlier and summed up in the intercept term. The only purpose of this particular experiment without the intercept term is to examine how stable the three elasticities α, β and γ have been during these two time periods. Once we have some idea of the stability we can go back to the original specifications of equation (3.10) and (3.11) for our second time period.

Another estimation problem is that the error term in the regression equation for our model may be thought of as a combination of many random events, and is itself a random event with normal distribution of zero mean and finite variance. The obvious constituents of this combination are some measure of fog, rainfall (which has been treated as an independent variable in the earlier section), snow and ice on the road, and, maybe, some measure of driver fatigue etc. Of all these random events, fog has some special consideration in our study. In some studies[13] it has been found that thick fog (visibility less than 200m) affects both traffic flow and casualties. This implies that the error term may not be totally independent of the independent variables. But the same studies indicate that 'thick fog occurs in Great Britain on about 10 days each year ...' (Moore, op. cit.) and 'generally, thick fog was found to be relatively infrequent, patchy, rarely widespread and of short duration. Its frequency inland has been falling in recent years, probably because of the Clean Air Act, 1956' (Codling, op. cit). Again, '... some two per cent of all road casualties occur in foggy weather ... and ... the total number of motorway fog accidents is small...' (Moore, op. cit). Because of this relative insignificance of fog on traffic flow and casualties on the motorways we may perhaps be allowed to disregard the possible relation between V and the error term, so far as the latter is influenced by the incidence of fog.

The results for our two-year models were presented above. First, we presented them without the intecept term in equation (3.10) for both the time periods. This may indicate the stability of the parameters during the period under study. Next, we presented the last period results in the form of both equation (3.10) and (3.11). The parameters in equation (3.10) would indicate the relevant elasticities whereas equation (3.11) could be used to assess the impact of the petrol crisis on casualties.

In Table 3.5, all the coefficients are significant at 95 per cent level of significance, whereas only γ in Table 3.6 for fatalities is not significantly different from zero. There is no positive indication of autocorrelation in either table, as in fact there is evidence of zero autocorrelation in some cases at both 1 per cent and 5 per cent significance levels. The parameters in the two tables are fairly close to imply there is not much structural

Table 3.5
Motorway casualties: log-linear regression equations without intercepts:
January 1970 to December 1971

Parameters Casualties	α	β	γ	R^2	D.W.
Fatal	2·614 (99·8)	1·053 (99·9)	−0·654 (99·7)	·400	2·04
Serious	1·515 (99·7)	1·286 (99·9)	−0·249 (95·5)	·378	1·75
Slight	1·729 (99·9)	1·498 (99·9)	−0·186 (98·1)	·711	1·96
Total	1·700 (99·9)	1·606 (99·9)	−0·222 (99·1)	·657	1·73

Table 3.6
Motorway casualties: log-linear regression equations without intercepts:
January 1972 to March 1974

Parameters Casualties	α	β	γ	R^2	D.W.
Fatal	2·218 (99·9)	0·810 (99·9)	−0·031 (12·8)	·560	1·47
Serious	1·536 (99·9)	1·301 (99·9)	−0·245 (97·4)	·630	1·79
Slight	1·877 (99·9)	1·533 (99·9)	−0·178 (93·7)	·800	0·95
Total	1·801 (99·9)	1·630 (99·9)	−0·205 (98·0)	·815	1·11

Table 3.7

Measures of neutrality of technical innovation from the previous two tables

Casualties	Ratio	$\dfrac{\beta}{\alpha}$	$\dfrac{\gamma}{\alpha}$	$\dfrac{\gamma}{\beta}$
Fatal		·40	—	—
		·37	—	—
Serious		·85	−·16	−·19
		·85	−·16	−·19
Slight		·87	−·11	−·12
		·82	−·10	−·12
Total		·95	−·13	−·14
		·91	−·11	−·13

change in the corresponding elasticities. This is confirmed in Table 3.7 where the values of the two successive periods for the relevant ratios are presented. The magnitudes in Tables 3.5 and 3.6, however, are not the proper elasticities to be used, because we have deliberately left out the intercept term for reasons described above. Having now established that the casualty relations have been fairly stable for the four years under review we now present the estimates of equations (3.10) and (3.11) for January 1972 to March 1974 in Tables 3.8 and 3.9.

The coefficients of Table 3.8 and Table 3.9 are all highly significant except for fatalities. There is hardly any sign of autocorrelation and the R^2s for Table 3.9 are substantially higher than the corresponding R^2s in Table 3.6. One notable feature of our experiment is that the coefficients in volume of traffic and average speed have been consistently well determined in all the four tables. As already mentioned, only results in Tables 3.8 and 3.9 could be used for some analysis of casualty relations. We can see from Table 3.9 that there is no sign of a learning process with respect to amount of driving and average speed — all the relevant parameters are greater than unity. This obviously implies that the more one drives on the motorways, the more one is proportionately likely to be involved in an accident. This is contrary to the results in all roads reported in the earlier section where there is definite evidence of a learning process. Similarly, the faster one drives on the motorways, the more one is proportionately likely to be an accident victim.

Table 3.8
Motorway casualties: linear equations for January 1972 to March 1974

Casualties	Intercept	α	β	γ	R^2	F	D.W.
Fatal	−56·68 (98·8)	35·21 (99·6)	0·81 (95·6)	−0·28 (25·9)	·618	9·70	2·11
Serious	−269·02 (99·8)	161·35 (99·9)	4·72 (99·7)	−6·90 (96·0)	·641	10·73	2·53
Slight	−809·47 (99·9)	532·93 (99·9)	12·43 (99·9)	−15·22 (96·7)	·813	26·14	1·69
Total	−1169·70 (99·9)	746·66 (99·9)	18·49 (99·9)	−24·60 (98·7)	·819	27·15	2·08

Table 3.9
Motorway casualties: log-linear equations for January 1972 to March 1974

Casualties	Intercept	α	β	γ	R^2	F	D.W.
Fatal	−14·81 (99·2)	1·73 (99·5)	4·45 (99·8)	−0·04 (14·8)	·711	14·78	2·06
Serious	−5·52 (92·3)	1·35 (99·9)	2·66 (99·9)	−0·25 (98·0)	·680	12·74	2·25
Slight	−6·00 (97·4)	1·68 (99·9)	3·01 (99·9)	−0·18 (95·7)	·841	31·79	1·28
Total	−5·41 (97·4)	1·62 (99·9)	2·96 (99·9)	−0·20 (98·8)	·853	34·75	1·58

(Numbers within brackets for Tables 3.5, 3.6, 3.8 and 3.9 indicate the appropriate significance levels.)

One application of the equations in Table 3.8 would be to calculate what would have happened if there were no petrol crisis. We already know that the equations for the periods before and after the crisis are comparable from our stable parameters in Tables 3.5 and 3.6. So we may be able to use equations in Table 3.8 to estimate the hypothetical casualty figures, assuming the rising trend in volume of traffic and average speed would have been maintained, with weather conditions remaining as they actually were. The difference between these estimated figures and the actual figures would then tell us the hypothetical savings of lives and limbs due to the extraneous disturbance. These figures are listed below.

Table 3.10
Hypothetical savings of lives and limbs on the motorways:
October 1973 to March 1974

Causes Casualties	Fall in V	Reduction in S	Totals
Fatalities	34	29	63
Serious	156	169	325
Slight	537	465	1,002
Total	727	663	1,390

It is apparent from the above numbers that the fall in V and the fall in S had almost equal effect on the fall in Xs during the experimental six months.[14]

In this section we have presented an aggregative model to estimate the effect on motorway casualties of traffic volume, speed and weather conditions. The first two were reduced through public policy during the winter of 1973–74, thus offering us a rare opportunity to conduct statistical experiment with our model. Generally, our results indicate that motorway casualties were relatively stable functions of these three factors — traffic volume, speed and weather conditions — during the four years, January 1970 to March 1974. More particularly, they also indicate that the fall in volume of traffic and speed on the motorways have been equally responsible for the reduction of casualty figures during the six experimental months of winter, 1973–74. This finding clearly has implications for government policy on motorway speed limits. But before we go on to use these results for a cost-benefit analysis of traffic speed in chapter 5, we present a theoretical basis of an economic analysis of personal injury from all kinds of accidents in the next chapter. This will provide us with the economic context of preventive and compensatory measures against accidental personal injury in general and thus help to formulate social policy in this area.

Notes

1 The formula is as follows:

$$D = 0{\cdot}0003\ (NP^2)$$

where, D = number of road fatalities
N = number of motor vehicles
P = population of the country under review
It is discussed in his two articles: (1) R.J. Smeed, (1949), op. cit.; (2) R.J. Smeed, (1972), op. cit.

2 A. Peranio, 'Conceptualisation and Use of Road Safety and Traffic Engineering Formulas', *Traffic Quarterly,* 1971, pp. 429–46.

3 R.M. Solow, 'Technical change and the aggregate production function', *The Review of Economics and Statistics,* vol. XXXIX, 1957, pp. 312–20.

4 'The most comprehensive study of the field of statistical accident research is probably that carried out by the German "HUK Verband" in which injuries in 1969 were evaluated and analysed according to 400 different aspects' 'An International Comparison of Road Accidents – causes, consequences, prevention', *Sigma,* no. 10–11, October–November 1963.

5 J.P. Bull and B.J. Roberts, 'Road Accident Statistics – A Comparison of Police and Hospital Information', *Accident Analysis and Prevention,* vol. 5, 1973, pp. 45–53.

6 We are indebted to Dr J.P. Bull for pointing out to us this limitation of the 'slight injuries' data.

7 The weight pattern is suggested by the Great Britain weather statistics for 1970 and 1971, published in RRL Report (LR 548).

8 Ministry of Transport, *How Fast,* HMSO, 1968.

9 D. Ghosh and D. Lees, 'Changing Patterns of Traffic and Weather Effects on Road Casualties in Great Britain,' Discussion Paper No. 1 in *Discussion Papers in Industrial Economics,* Department of Industrial Economics, University of Nottingham, September 1974.

10 D. Ghosh, D. Lees and W. Seal, 'Effects of Traffic Flows and Speed on Motorway Casualties in Great Britain, January 1972 to March 1974', Discussion Paper no. 8 in *Discussion Papers in Industrial Economics,* Department of Industrial Economics, University of Nottingham, October 1974.

11 Ministry of Transport, (op. cit.).

12 These measures are taken from: L.W. Ackroyd and M. Bettison, 'Vehicle Speeds on the M1 in Nottinghamshire', *Traffic Engineering and Control,* January 1974, and C.C. Wright, 'A New Technique for Estimating Motorway Speeds and Some Results Obtained under the Emergency 50 m.p.h. Limit', Institute of Highway Engineers, October 1974.

13 P.J. Codling, 'Thick fog and its effects on traffic flow and accidents,' *TRRL Report* LR 377, 1971; R.L. Moore and L. Cooper, 'Fog and Road Traffic.' *TRRL Report* LR 446, 1972.

14 D. Ghosh, D. Lees and W. Seal, 'Death on the Motorway', *New Society,* 22 August 1974.

4 Towards a social policy

4.1 Introduction

In the previous chapter we concentrated on the analysis of the statistical material in order to identify some of the technical relationships contributing to the accident phenomenon. Although we have applied economic techniques, we cannot regard our studies as attempting to confront the essence of the economic problem. The identification of the accident relationships is a necessary step towards the development of a social policy but it is not sufficient. In this chapter we propose to tackle some of the more strictly economic issues by deriving an accident policy from economic theory. While in later chapters we will present more operational and empirical analysis, our present purpose is to build up an overview of the economic approach to accidental personal injury.

In sections 4.1.2–4.1.7 inclusive we intend to review the policy issues and particularly show how the aims of a social policy emerge from the ethical and methodological underpinnings of economic theory. In 4.2.2 we develop a model which synthesises many of the ideas discussed in earlier sections. Many of the concepts will receive only an introductory treatment. It is hoped that the reader will increase his understanding of them by relating them to the more detailed and empirically orientated material presented in the rest of the book.

4.2 Policy objectives

A truly comprehensive treatment of personal injury would include a section on intentional wounding and killing. We have chosen to concentrate on *accidental* injury where the relationship between the victim and the injurer is less obvious or even completely absent. Although accidents are by definition unexpected and unintentional, they are unlikely to be regarded as 'acts of God'. The stock response to both the routine accident toll on the highways and the more spectacular disaster is not usually one of fatalistic acceptance but is rather more likely to attempt to ascertain the cause or causes. It is, of course, but a short step from the identification of a cause to a demand for prevention.

The polar opposite to the fatalistic attitude of 'accidents will happen' is probably the notion that accidents can and should be totally eliminated. Such an extreme position may sound unappealing when stated baldly but it does seem to be a logical extension of some fashionable views on accident prevention.[1] As with demand for full and universal compensation for accident victims, such apparently compassionate and humane views undoubtedly receive widespread approval in the prevailing ethos of a welfare state.

As economists, we must be prepared to accept the disapproval of those whose overtly charitable opinions seem to us to reveal either, at best, an unrealistic view of human nature and a careless analysis of the social choice problem or, at worst, the hypocrisy of the special pleader (see Tullock[2]).

A glance across the range of literature on accident analysis suggests to us that the attitude towards accident prevention is to some extent a function of the discipline of the researcher. Thus the medic may be expected to be more concerned with accident elimination than, for example, the highway engineer who is generally faced with a complex mix of objectives. While most professional accident researchers recognise the effect of resource constraints on accident elimination, it is probable that the economist's most natural ally in this area of policy objectives is the lawyer. Let us explain this assertion.

In countries, such as the USA and the UK, whose legal system is based on Anglo-Saxon traditions, accidents frequently invoke civil litigation. The motivation for the litigation arises from a desire on behalf of the victim to obtain financial compensation for his injuries. The legal basis of any award he receives is usually the principle of negligence under which the court investigates the pre-accident behaviour of both the defendant and the plaintiff. As legal precedents have been set, the civil law on personal injury or the tort system, as it is usually known, together with some statutory measures, has become an important institutional device for defining the social rules determining behaviour between individuals. Under the negligence concept, the court does not expect an ideal level of 'total' safety but tests whether the parties conformed to an objective level of care. We will expand on the aims and methods of the tort system throughout the book.[3] Our main aim at this stage is to suggest that lawyers both in their academic role and in their capacity as legal practitioners do not envisage extreme solutions such as either the complete elimination of accidents or comprehensive compensation.

Having stressed the similarity of outlook between economists and lawyers, we do feel that it is the economist who has a special responsibility for, and a comparative advantage in, analysing the individual and social choice problems involved in the formation and implementation of a social policy for personal injury. The economist assumes that the individual has many objectives. In economic jargon, he assumes that the individual maximises a utility function in which there are a multitude of goods and that if, for example, he wishes to have more safety, then he must sacrifice quantities of other goods. In short, the economist's approach is based on attaining an *optimal* rather than a zero level of accidents. While the individual optimisation process is trivial,(and for our purposes, uninteresting) as we shall see in the next section, the development of *socially* optimal policies is strewn with ethical and methodological problems. We aim to minimise these problems by explicitly stating our basic value judgements. We do not pretend, however, that this process will pre-empt all controversy since much of the theoretical disagreement is concerned with the definition of optimality and sub-optimality in specific real world situations. It is hoped, however, that we may avoid the worst of the confusion evident for example, in the debates over the tort system where many of the most sterile arguments can be attributed to a haphazard specification of policy objectives [but see note 4.]

The main emphasis in this chapter will be on the economics of accident prevention. As we shall see, we cannot, *theoretically,* separate accident deterrence from the compensation of the victims. For the moment, we will justify this emphasis by assuming firstly, that the *empirical* relationship between accident prevention and compensation may not be as significant as our theory suggests. Secondly, we treat the objective of compensation as one of loss-spreading rather than cost-shifting and as such give it separate treatment in chapter 7.

4.2.1 *Some ethical and methodological issues*

In order to specify a socially optimal policy it is necessary to review briefly the methodological and ethical basis of economic theory. We do not regard this basis as wholly immutable. Indeed we will relax some of its more extreme requirements in the interests of analytical ease both in our theoretical modelling and in our quantitative work. It is important, however, to be aware of what the benefits of rigour and operationality cost in terms of philosophical purity.

One methodological plank, at least nominally adhered to by non-Marxist economists, is the assumption that the individual is the fundamental philosophical entity. In more specific terms, this may mean that as a normative proposition the individual may be assumed to be the best judge of his own welfare or, alternatively, it may be asserted as a factual premise that the individual is the only person in any position to be able to evaluate it. Either way, the implication is that welfare is a subjective experience and inseparable from the individual. Given this individualistic postulate, when an economist talks about 'society' he does not view it as an organic entity with a personality of its own but as a collection of all individuals comprising the group.

The difficulties inherent in this view of society become apparent when, in the design of a social policy, we require some method of establishing how particular changes in the social state affect social welfare and thereby how we can judge when society is in the 'optimal', or best possible, position. The classical utilitarian 'solved' this problem by assuming that in principle it was possible to compare alternative social states by aggregating individual utilities and that the objective of policy was to maximise the sum of individual utilities. The strict Paretian approach rejects any arbitrary system of aggregation of utilities although its quantitative offspring cost-benefit analysis does involve an aggregation process (see section 4.2.5). Changes are evaluated with the use of a lower order value judgement which avoids the necessity of comparing or aggregating individual utilities. This value judgement states that if after a particular change at least one person is better off as he views it and no one is worse off as they view their welfare then such a change is considered to constitute an unambiguous increase in welfare (see Sen[5] for a more rigorous and complete analysis of the Pareto criterion).

It is often argued that the Paretian value judgement is unduly restricting since it is hard to envisage many social changes which do not involve at least one person losing. Free market enthusiasts would argue that this overlooked the unique social role of the market where individuals are continually exchanging goods and services to their *mutual* advantage. It is clearly this ethical property of market exchange which makes the allocation of resources through competitive markets seem such an appealing institution to many economists (see especially Buchanan[6]). Another and related weakness of the Pareto criterion is its inability to point to a uniquely preferred social ordering which has somewhat unfairly given it a reputation for favouring the status quo. In fact, it is logically perfectly possible for any distribution of goods and services between individuals to be Pareto optimal, however just or unjust a 'reasonable' and compassionate observer may adjudge a particular distribution to be. Or, as Sen puts it: 'an economy can be optimal in this (Paretian) sense even when some people are rolling in luxury and others are near starvation as long as the starvers cannot be made better off without cutting into the pleasures of the rich.'

Apart from facilitating Pareto-permissible moves, smoothly operating markets are also useful devices for generating data on individual preferences. Although we have already stated that welfare is ultimately a subjective phenomenon, it is common methodology for economists (though not all, see e.g. Buchanan[7]) to make inferences about individual preferences on the basis of the choices that individuals make in the market place. Thus if an individual is prepared to voluntarily give up a quantity of a particular entity in exchange for another entity we may infer, firstly, that since it was a voluntary move by both parties to the transaction welfare has increased and, secondly, that the exchange may have revealed an objective measure of individual valuation in terms of a numeraire commodity. Since market generated data usually form an important part of cost-benefit studies, we will return to the particular problems of valuation in accident policy in later chapters.

Given the ends of orthodox welfare economics, it is easy to appreciate the crucial role that the market as an institution plays in economic analysis. It is, therefore, relatively easy to see why, when economists seek to justify institutional change, particularly some form of collective action, they begin by attempting to identify instances of 'market failure'.

4.2.2 *Market failure: accident externalities and the theory of public goods*

One much quoted source of market failure stems from what are known as external effects or externalities. Calabresi[8] has justly criticised the lack of precision in the use of the externality argument and feels that: 'such terms as external social costs and benefits . . . are not self-defining and are, in fact, as narrow or as broad as any society cares to make them.'

Before we consider the validity of such a criticism, let us base our argument on Meade's[9] definition of an external (dis)economy which he defines as: 'an event which confers an appreciable benefit (inflicts appreciable damage) on some person or persons who were not fully consenting parties in reaching the decision or decisions which led directly or indirectly to the event in question.'

This is a useful definition since it is easily related to accidental interaction. For example, if a pedestrian is knocked down in a motor accident, we may plausibly postulate that an externality relationship can be identified. In other words, the external effect relates to a particular event. We may contrast this with other definitions where the externality relationship concerns *continuing* activities. Thus Buchanan and Stubblebine[10] define an externality to be present when an individual A's utility function is described thus:

$$u^A = u^A(X_1, X_2, \ldots, X_m, Y_1)$$

where Y_1 is an activity which is under the control of a second individual, B. It is harder to relate this definition to the accident situation since there may be some difficulty in perceiving the external cost creating activity, Y_1. Thus, in the popular example of the smoking factory chimney, it is relatively easy to identify a particular harmful effect. It is considerably less easy to identify the form of the externality relationship between, for example, motorists or between motorists and pedestrians. If we adopt an ex ante approach, then we may suggest that one individual may be imposing an external cost by increasing the *probability* of an accident occurring to other persons. Clearly, there may be problems in the perception of such an externality relationship. It is consequently easy to see why accident externality models are so frequently based on the ex post approach of the tort system where both the costs and the relationships appear to be so much more tangible.

We may generalise this observation by suggesting that the tort system has become a sort of pedagogical device in the economic literature on accident externalities. Thus if it is difficult to envisage an ex ante accident externality relationship, it is intuitively much easier to envisage an externality if we have a device which makes an ex post *moral* decision to bring certain individuals together in a situation where one party is the victim and the other party is the injurer.

The danger of using the civil liability situation as an illustration of externalities is that the issue of who is imposing costs on whom will tend to be prejudged by the analyst. This is one of Coase's[11] criticisms of Pigou's[12] analysis of the divergence between private cost and social cost. While Pigou assumed that the smoky factory imposed an external cost on the neighbouring laundry, Coase pointed out that the externality relationship was reciprocal and that the court's specific job was to decide who had the right to do what. Similarly in our own example, it would be erroneous (or moralistic) to suggest B is 'imposing' accident costs on A since it is the court's problem in a negligence case to decide between the two parties.

Brown[13] suggests that accidents should be regarded as 'joint products'. Thus an accident is not caused by either the injurer or the victim but is a joint product of both parties. He feels that: 'The only role for discussions of causation is to exonerate a party completely by proving that he is a stranger to the accident.'[14]

If we for the moment ignore the problems of perception and evaluation of accident costs, we may illustrate the two party accident relationship with an externality model often used by economists to analyse the adversary procedure of the legal process.[15, 16, 17] In Figure 4.1 A's

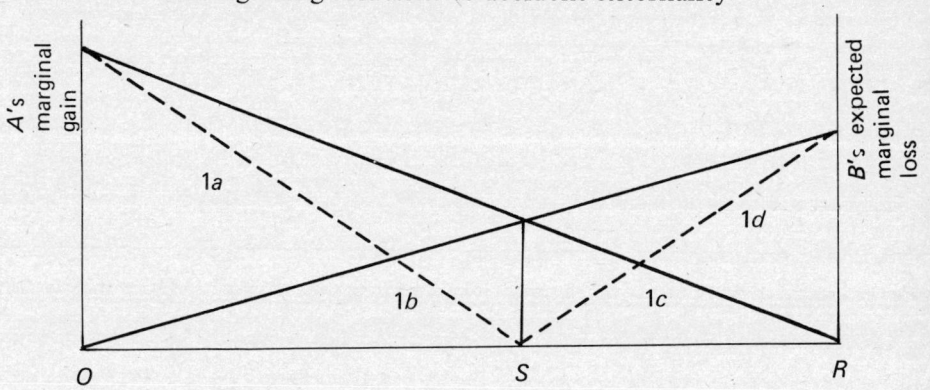

Figure 4.1
Bargaining solutions to accident externality

activity is generating gains to him at a diminishing marginal rate and causing (expected) losses to B at an increasing marginal rate.

The diagram illustrates two polar positions at O and R and an optimum position at OS. OS is the optimal position in the sense that the combined gain is greater at this point than at either of the polar positions O and R. Having set up this hypothetical relationship and established a point of maximum gain, we may consider alternative devices for attaining OS. Coase showed using numerical examples that as long as bargaining was costless, and ignoring wealth effects, it did not matter whether the courts awarded the legal right to either A or B. This may also be seen from the diagram. If A has the right to continue his activity then B still has the incentive to bribe A to move to position OS. B would be willing to pay up to $1c + 1d$ while A would be prepared to accept as little as $1c$. If B has the right (i.e. A is restrained by a court injunction) then A could take up position OS by paying $1b$ to B and still gain $1a$.[18]

If, however, bargaining costs preclude a market adjustment then there may be a role for a non-market institution to impose a marginal tax-subsidy scheme. The tax-subsidy rate will be set so that A's gain and B's loss are equated at zero. In Figure 4.1 the dotted lines represent the adjusted marginal curves. Some economists have naturally seen the courts' imposition of damages and payments of compensation as approximating this ideal tax-subsidy process (see e.g. Posner[19] and Burrows[20]).

Whatever our reservations are about this representation of the tort system, our model illustrates very clearly that OS is not a unique optimum in the Paretian sense defined in section 4.2.1. Thus when the courts make a decision on rights they are forced to make a choice on the distribution of wealth between individuals. Let us expand on this problem by considering the frequently discussed situation of asymmetrical bargaining costs. The court may be faced with the choice of awarding a property right to either A or B where, because of lower bargaining costs, community gain is maximised by making a decision in favour of A. Thus in an extreme case, high bargaining costs may 'anchor' the solution at O if B is given the right whereas if A has the right then bargaining results in the attainment of OS (see Figure 4.1). This does not necessarily mean that the court should award the right to A on pure efficiency grounds since the choice clearly redistributes wealth from B to A. Thus, to summarise, although we may be able to identify an area of market failure in situations where property rights are ill defined, we must accept that any delineation of property rights has distributional as well as efficiency implications. In section 4.2.4 we will attempt to come to terms with distributional problems. In the meantime, however, we will postulate an externality situation where the externalities are Pareto relevant and thereby more unambiguously indicative of market failure.

Let us assume a situation where the basic human and property rights are already defined. This means that the 'consumer' of a harmful effect accepts that the existing assignment of rights does not give him any legal recourse and that he is prepared to bribe the 'producer' of the harmful effect to modify his behaviour. Let us further assume that there are many such 'consumers' who are also prepared to bribe the 'producer'. It is possible that the externality is not internalised by individual voluntary action because each consumer is in a 'free rider' situation. This means that it is more rational for the individual consumer to attempt to obtain a free-ride by securing benefits which are paid for by someone else. Since ,this is the optimal strategy for each individual the theory implies that certain types of joint consumption goods will not be produced in optimal quantities. The interesting point about this second externality is that it does not (in principle, at least) run into the distributional problems of the small number—liability situations. Unexploited gains from trade between consumers and producers of the external effect persist because of the *large numbers* involved not because of an unwillingness of one party to bribe the other.

With the introduction of the 'paradox of isolation' we have posed the accident policy issue as a part of a general problem of public goods. Practical examples of public goods are notoriously vulnerable to criticisms since most goods (and 'bads') are somewhere on a spectrum between the polar points of the pure private good and the pure public good. If, for example, we treat road safety as an economic good then it is relatively easy to envisage that individual bargaining between motorists is unlikely to occur and that the desired 'quantity' of safety must to some extent be provided through a public agency. On the other hand, the individual may also make *private* choices on, for example, the fitting of safety tyres and the level of passenger protection offered by different brands of car.

Although we suggested that the bargaining problem is specifically a problem of large numbers, we may illustrate the joint consumption characteristic of the public good in Figure 4.2 using a two-person model. The diagram may be regarded as a triangular Edgeworth box which incorporates Shibata's presentation of bargaining possibilities[21] along with a treatment of the *production* possibilities. On the horizontal axis we have the public good X_n which in the case of, for example, a motor crash barrier is jointly consumed by two motorists, A and B. On the vertical axis we have the community endowment in terms of numeraire commodity, (X_j). *BC* represents the group's production possibility curve. *DE* represents A's production possibility curve using A's initial endowment while *DF* represents B's production possibility curve assuming that only B's initial endowment is available. A's indifference curves are represented by continuous curves convex to origin A; B's curves by the broken lines convex to origin B. It may be seen from the diagram that both individuals may attain a preferred position if the public good (X_n) is jointly financed. That is, both individuals can go beyond their *individual* production possibility curves (*DE* and *DF*).

If we compare Figure 4.2 with Figure 4.1, we can see how the public goods externality is at least potentially Pareto relevant. In Figure 4.2 the starting point for the notional 'negotiations' is point D from which it is possible for both A and B to move to preferred positions in *DECF*. In Figure 4.1 we assumed that since it is the *initial* delineation of property rights which is in dispute we cannot characterise the externality relationship between A and B as Pareto relevant until a decision on the rights assignment has been made. In other words, in the 'pure' efficiency approach we must assume that the courts or some other non-market institution fix a starting point at either O or R on the basis of non-Paretian value judgements and that a willingness to trade emerges after this assignment of rights.

Figure 4.2 also illustrates the consequences of relaxing the assumption of constant marginal utilities of income upon which the validity of the Coase theorem depends. If this condition held then the contract locus (*VW*) would be a vertical line with the implication that the distribution issue (i.e. the division of X_j) may be treated independently from the allocational problem (i.e. the production of X_n). In Figure 4.2 *VW* is not vertical and therefore 'wealth effects' do have allocational implications.

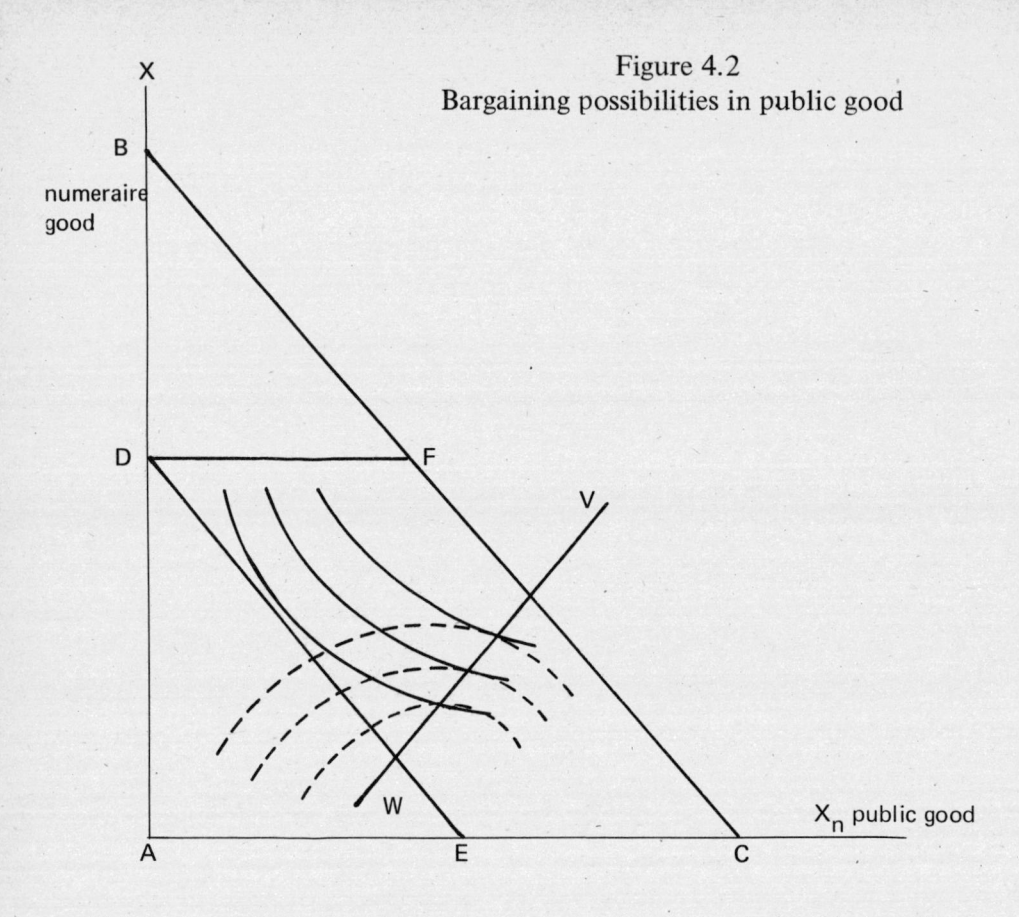

Figure 4.2
Bargaining possibilities in public good

Although we have suggested that some policy issues in accident policy may be presented as a public goods problem, it is not clear how the *potential* Paretian gains we have identified may be realised by a particular institutional arrangement. We have ruled out individual bargaining by positing a free-rider situation but we cannot suggest an alternative non-market institution capable of solving the problems in an optimal manner. The theory of public goods is frequently interpreted as the intellectual basis for collective activity by which the individual is coerced into financing the public good. Although we may ensure that at least some of the public good is provided through collective action, we cannot assume a priori that collective decision-making will reveal the individual marginal evaluations necessary to compute the optimal output. Buchanan and Tullock[22] have shown that a collective decision made on the basis of simple majority rule may merely replace one set of externalities by a new set although they do suggest that 'log-rolling' or vote-trading may contribute to optimal decision-making in the long run.

In general, it may be seen that we cannot expect clear policy implications from theoretical welfare economics. We can model the accident externality and suggest the existence of potential Paretian gains. We cannot, however, use our theory to specify a particular institutional device. In section 4.2.5 we consider how some economists and lawyers have attempted to apply a less theoretical and more pragmatic allocative norm. However, before we abandon the pure Paretian approach, let us first consider how we may handle the problem of equity which theoretical welfare economics, simultaneously, highlights and evades.

4.2.3 *Formal justice and substantive justice*

One policy objective we did not mention in 4.2 is the professed legal objective of accident law; that is, the goal of 'justice'. Criticisms that the tort system is inefficient in its administration of compensation funds (see chapter 7) are often countered by lawyers with the assertion that the extra costs are the inevitable high price society must pay for justice. It is apparent, however, that the lawyer's concept of justice can be so all-embracing that it subsumes most of the desired characteristics of a social policy. It is, therefore, not surprising that the criteria of a 'just' framework of accident law is unclear even to lawyers. Many lawyers evade the issue by substituting a moral approach to the law by a positive approach which attempts to ask 'what is the law?' rather than 'what should the law be?'

The positive approach does have one useful attribute in that it helps us to distinguish between formal justice and substantive justice. Thus, formal justice does not ask 'what is (or should be) the moral basis of the law?' — it merely refers to the ability of the institution administering the law to provide consistent treatment of similar cases, or, in other words, to treat 'like cases alike'. Substantive justice, on the other hand is concerned with the broad moral principles underlying the law. Thus it is concerned with the economy-wide distribution of income and wealth and the *general principles* governing social relations. Economists have traditionally concentrated on issues of substantive justice since their preoccupation is with the general distribution of income in contrast to the courts which, on the surface at least, consider only the distribution between individuals on a case-by-case basis. More recently, there has been a growing realisation among economists that the distribution of utility is a function not only of the distribution of goods but also of the property rights defining how these goods may be used.

In distinguishing between formal justice and substantive justice, we may have given the impression that we expect a clear 'division of labour' between different institutions on the different forms of justice. For example, we might expect the courts to be solely interested in the administration of formal justice while issues of substantive justice are resolved through the political process. We cannot, however, differentiate institutional roles in this manner since in countries operating an Anglo-Saxon based legal system, many property rights, including some with direct relevance to accident law, have evolved through judgements made in the courts. In other words, although lawyers may try to limit their interest to achieving 'justice as regularity' they are involved in a social institution which has unavoidably had to tangle with issues of substantive justice. Thus, if in the individual tort case, the lawyers apparently limit their discussion to the facts of the case and the legal precedents, the moral basis of these precedents is usually the principle of negligence. The positive approach to the law clearly evades the key policy issues in accident law for as Rawls[23] points out, formal justice is a necessary feature of a 'just' society but it is not sufficient.

Rawls also stresses that theories of substantive justice are not concerned with the problems of non-compliance. A case could be made out that the courts' whole *raison d'être* is to tackle the particular problems raised by non-compliance or in other words the non-observation of property rights. It would therefore be fallacious to criticise the justice achieved by the courts in a partially compliant society where legitimate expectations are uncertain and property rights are not always observed by comparing it with an ideal concept of justice worked out in the context of a fully compliant society. In the same way that we shall modify our objective of efficiency, we may compromise on our absolute principles of justice. But before we consider compromise, we aim to present a 'pure' goal of justice in the same spirit as our 'pure' goal of efficiency in the belief that an over hasty rejection of theoretical ideals would seem to limit unnecessarily the basis of possible reforms.

While any prescriptive theory must ultimately be based on value judgements, it seems intuitively plausible that a consensus orientated value-judgement is preferable to a more controversial one. This is clearly the reason for the economists' persistence with the Paretian definition of a social improvement. As Sen[24] puts it: 'If everyone agrees on a certain value-judgement, the fact that it cannot be verified may not cause any great commotion.'

Buchanan[25] suggests that the unanimity rule may be used to decide on the more basic, constitutional problems which he himself stresses must be answered before consideration of Paretian efficiency can emerge. The difficulty with his approach is that since his starting point for consensus formation seems to be the status quo we might expect an arbitrary and conservative bias to any decisions on rules and distributions that are made. Given an existing distribution of human and property rights, it would seem probable that some individuals have a vested interest in maintaining particular social rules, and the probability of reaching full consensus on basic constitutional issues might be expected to be fairly low. If, however, we envisage a 'state of ignorance' in which a particular individual does not know his future status in society we may be able to derive certain basic principles of justice by deducing what self-interested individuals would agree on in this hypothetical 'contractarian' situation. Rawls suggests that the outcome of this sort of 'thought experiment' would be a 'maximin' concept of justice and that attention will be directed to the worst-off individual in society.

While nobody would expect a theory of justice to suggest precise levels of compensation for personal injury or help the courts decide on what sort of behaviour constitutes the 'due level of care'. as with the Pareto criterion in considerations of efficiency, we are provided with a relatively unambiguous yardstick with which to appraise the broad principles of justice underlying a particular social institution. One way in which to approach *specific* policy issues is to consider whether a particular institution such as the courts is a plausible source of consensus orientated values. Since the essence of the judicial decision is its *independence* from political pressure, it may seem at first sight that the 'undemocratic' nature of judicial decision-making weakens its ability to interpret consensus values. On the other hand, supporters of court based law suggest that the very absence of pressure on the judge allows the court to base its decision on general Kantian principles. Their suspicion is directed towards statute law which frequently seems to reflect the success of powerful lobbies rather than principles which maximise the social good (see Tullock[26] and chapter 7 where we return to this debate).

Another way by which we can explicitly introduce distributional value judgements is to incorporate distributional weights into our cost-benefit calculations. In this broad distributional sense, it is reasonable to argue that the economics approach is relatively 'value free' since it is possible, at least in principle, to base one's calculation on any preferred system of weights. The fact that a unitary weighting system where a pound to one (poor) man is worth the same to another (rich) man is so frequently used is more a matter of convenience and the lack of a theoretically based alternative, than evidence of a particularly conservative ethical stance by the analyst. These certainly are the reasons behind the use of a unitary weighting system in our own cost–benefit calculus in the next chapter.

4.2.4 *Ignorance, uncertainty and the economics of information*

In the previous section we argued that the economic approach to social policy may not solve the problem of distributional justice but it cannot be said either to ignore it or to bias decisions in favour of the status quo. Another common criticism of economic methodology is its basis on the principle of consumer sovereignty or, in other words, the belief that the individual is the best/sole judge of his own welfare. This criticism is particularly prevalent in the area of social policy where much of the legislation and much of the provision of services seem to have a strong paternalistic element. It is easy to find examples of product bans and restrictive legislation, which are clearly designed to 'protect' the individual from taking particular risks. We cannot automatically condemn such measures as élitist or illiberal since once we admit ignorance into our economic model, there may be 'economic' reasons for accepting them. Before we explore this last statement let us first consider the role of uncertainty.

Many economists have not distinguished sufficiently between the response to uncertainty and the possible response to ignorance. Hirschleifer[27] suggests that: '*Uncertainty* is summarised by the dispersion of individuals' subjective probability (or belief) distribution over possible states of the world. *Information* .... consists of events tending to change these probability distributions.'

Thus faced with uncertainty the individual may attempt to maximise *expected* utility, with devices such as gambling and insurance. Faced with ignorance, the individual may engage in an active search for information which leads to a change in his belief distribution.

A social policy for accidents is concerned with both passive adaptation to uncertainty and the active adaptation of information production and distribution. Since we characterise much of the policy debate in chapter 7 on loss-spreading as an example of passive adaptation to uncertainty, our main concern in this section will be to review the economics of information search.

One possible policy approach is to consider whether information, and particularly accident information, has any special characteristics that indicate a particular mode of production and dissemination. As with other economic goods, it is costly to produce and to distribute. Goldberg[28] suggests that it is cheaper to disseminate if it is communicated via product basis and regulatory legislation: 'Enlarging the pool of product safety knowledge does not necessarily improve the welfare of the consumer, if the consumer is not accessible; and getting the information from the producer to the consumer is not a simple task. Information might be conveyed by banning certain products or by adopting specific liability rules.'

Clearly, the implication of the above argument is that there may be 'economic' reasons i.e. reasons consistent with the individualistic values of economies, for introducing restrictive legislation. The argument suggests that the individual finds it cheaper to delegate some decisions to an expert. As it is evident that even the most rugged individualist willingly delegates some decisions to specialists, such as doctors, we may expect a certain level of imposed decision-making to be acceptable. It is also evident, however, that the exact line of demarcation between voluntary delegation and unnecessary paternalism is a subject of fierce debate (see e.g. Oi's[29] reply to Goldberg).

Another feature of information is that it is to some extent a public good with the implication that, as we pointed out above, the private market may underprovide it. This argument is more usually applied to problems of promoting research into product innovation although the difficulty of setting up private property rights in accident information is clearly similar. Furthermore, once it is produced, the acquisition of knowledge by one individual does not reduce the amount available for other individuals. With these arguments in mind, even the more *laissez-faire* economist might favour at least some public production of information about accident risks.

Accident information may be costly to acquire but it is usually cheaper to collect after the event rather than before it. In other words, knowledge of accident causation is frequently based on the analysis of a particular disaster rather than on a predetermined series of tests. This point is well illustrated by the thalidomide case in which the knowledge concerning the damage to the foetus was only acquired after a calamitous international tragedy.

Demsetz[30] has suggested that the lower information costs attached to identifying losers after the event gives some justification to the court practice of ex post compensation. While it is clear that the compensation paid to losers is a more accurate reflection of their subjective costs if it is determined on the basis of voluntary agreement in the market, the 'second-best' solution in a world of high information costs may be to compensate the victims of an accident after they have been 'identified' by the accident. This particular economic rationalisation of injury compensation is reinforced by the courts' practice of applying an ex ante rather than an ex post standard of care. Thus, instead of being 'wise after the event', the courts will attempt to define an objective level of care to be conformed to by a 'reasonable' man. The defendant will not be found negligent on the basis of the ex post information available to the court since the courts have to be satisfied that the accident was 'foreseeable' by their hypothetical reasonable man.

In a similar spirit, a social policy for accidents should be concerned with setting an ex ante level of information production. While we clearly cannot suggest what the optimal provision of information should be, we might be able to compare institutional environments in an attempt to discover *whose* preferences are counting in each situation. In chapter 6 we will return to the problem of information in the context of product liability where we will consider the policy alternatives in a more empirical setting.

4.2.5 *The 'new' law and economics*

In this section we abandon the strict Paretian approach and consider the philosophically less pure but considerably more operational application of economic analysis followed by Calabresi and other students of what is sometimes known as the 'new' law and economics.[31] As long as we operate with a tough specification of optimality as defined in section 4.2.1, it is clear that our prescriptive range will be severely restricted. The Pareto criterion encourages the search for possible 'gains from trade' and in this respect it may be surprisingly critical of institutional obstacles to bargaining. However, the applicability of our approach is considerably widened if we modify our efficiency objective to the achievement of what are known as 'potential' Paretian improvements. These are changes in which the gainers would be able to compensate the losers and still be better off. But since no compensation is expected to be paid, an *unambiguous* improvement cannot be identified.

The potential Paretian improvement provides the theoretical basis for the empirical part of welfare economics usually known as cost–benefit analysis. The scientific purity of the cost–benefit approach has been criticised by those economists who are reluctant to give any normative value to attempts to express welfare in terms of a numeraire commodity. Buchanan[32], for example, feels that the prescriptive power of free market exchange is based on a direct link between subjective cost facing the individual and the choices he makes. He is consequently suspicious of attempts to derive normative implications from ex post market data along the lines suggested in 4.2.1. Similarly, McKean[33] in a cautious specification of his objective, illustrates the tentative nature of the conclusions one can expect from the economic analysis of liability assignments:

> I shall attempt, not to identify optimal policies, but simply to discuss some of the consequences of alternative products liability arrangements ... These consequences will be mainly certain costs generated by the alternative arrangements — costs in terms of the price tags that are implicit in a predominantly voluntary exchange system and that would help direct one toward Pareto optimal policies.

The assumption common to all studies in the new law and economics is that since transactions costs are a fact of life, the assignment of rights *does* affect the allocation of resources. Furthermore, it is assumed that the behavioural implications of different rights assignments can be predicted with the standard behavioural assumptions of positive economics. Thus the 'new' law and economics does not assume that individuals are automatically law abiding. It does assume that utility maximising individuals will respond in a predictable way to changes in incentives even if the incentives are not expressed in conventional economic entities (see e.g. G.S. Becker[34]).

Although we have bracketed Calabresi with the other students of law and economics, it is doubtful whether he would apply economic reasoning to the same extent as, for example, Becker has done. Let us illustrate this assertion with a brief review of Calabresi's concepts. Calabresi puts forward two main systems of accident control. His 'specific deterrence' system refers to regulations and product bans imposed collectively and enforced by criminal penalties. He stresses that there are some non-economic, moral values underlying such rules. On the other hand, his 'general deterrence' system is much more closely based on economic rationale. The aim of the system is to 'internalise' the costs of accidents inside the activities that generate them. Thus there is no moral ban on any individual engaging in an activity. He must, however, be prepared to pay the 'full cost' of participating where the full costs include the usual economic costs plus expected accident costs. The accident costs are as much as possible themselves based on individual valuations in the market.

In a system of general deterrence, we have to decide which activities should bear the accident costs. As we have noted earlier, accidents may frequently be regarded as 'joint products' and questions as to which party 'caused' the accident are misleading.[35] Calabresi suggests that liability should be imposed on the 'cheapest accident avoider'. He illustrates his concept with numerical examples which show how changes in liability affect the total sum of the costs of the accident and the costs of avoiding the accident.[36]

Most economists would agree that the loss *minimisation* objective is acceptable since it is logically equivalent to welfare *maximisation*. Given this objective, the methodology of the market deterrence approach seems to be that the preferred liability rule is chosen by comparing the aggregate costs of alternative rights assignments and choosing the assignment with the lowest costs. These costs include not only accident costs but also all the costs associated with either directly avoiding the accident or bribing others to avoid them. They also crucially include information costs entailed in assessing the accident probabilities.

In terms of theoretical welfare economics, Calabresi's market control has a number of weaknesses. First, the decision rule is based on comparing total costs rather than marginal costs. Second, the approach ignores the problem of the subjective nature of economic costs by assuming that a third party can estimate not only accident costs but also some of the more intangible transactions costs. On the other hand, the common sense appeal of the approach is clear. It does, for example, seem more likely that the effect of economic incentives to reduce road accidents will be greater if liability is imposed on the motorist rather than on the general taxpayer. Thus on the basis of a 'rough guess', Calabresi suggests that costs of road accidents should be borne by the motorist. In other words, although the concept of the least cost accident avoider may be difficult to define in general theoretical terms, it is often easy to identify a liability rule that would intuitively lead to a reduction in introspectively calculated total costs. Recent attempts to formalise Calabresi's ideas (see, for example, P.A. Diamond[37]) have highlighted some ambiguities but are a long way from arriving at any policy relevant solutions. As we shall see in chapter 6 with our discussions of product liability, the simplifications necessary for formal argument do not always form a very useful platform for policy discussions.

4.3 An economic theory of accident occurrence and prevention

In the next section, we present a model of accidental injury which incorporates many of the features of the approach outlined in the last section. Following Calabresi, we derive our normative implications by using an aggregative loss minimisation function.[38]

Unlike Calabresi, however, we are not concerned with the important problem of allocation of resources *between* activities since our model considers only a single activity and does not analyse the source of either compensation or expenditure on accident prevention. The model[39] draws heavily on the theorems developed in 'Crime and Punishment: an economic approach' in which Becker (op. cit.) applied price theory to analyse the 'demand' and 'supply' of offences. We use a similar approach to derive 'demand' and 'supply' curves of accidents. Although fundamentally a normative theory, we test some of the hypotheses underlying our behavioural assumptions using data on industrial accidents in the UK. The theory does not limit itself to considering 'what should the law be?' It incorporates decisions on enforcement of the law as well as non-legal accident reducing policy instruments such as motorway crash barriers and seat belts.

4.2.1 *The model*

Let X represent the level of potentially dangerous activity during a period of time and I stand for 'pain and suffering'[40] that participants in that activity are expected to sustain from personal injuries in it. X could be the production of coal during a week or it could be the volume of traffic during a month. Whatever I represents, it may be assumed that pain and suffering due to probable injury varies positively with X. Thus we have

$$I = I(X) \text{ and } I' > 0 \qquad (4.1)$$

A potentially dangerous activity like driving is also beneficial to the participants otherwise the activity will not be undertaken. If B stands for the benefit from such activity, we assume that

$$B = B(X) \text{ and } B' > 0 \qquad (4.2)$$

The net damage (D) from a level of X may now be defined as:

$$D(X) = I(X) - B(X) \qquad (4.3)$$

It may be further assumed that marginal pain and suffering from injury increases and marginal benefit diminishes with increase in the level of X. Thus we have

$$D''(X) = I''(X) - B''(X) > 0 \qquad (4.4)$$

The sign of marginal net damage from X i.e. $D'(X)$ is however, ambiguous since $I'(X)$ and $B'(X)$ are both positive.

Let us now look into other aspects of social loss from preventing and sustaining accidental personal injuries. Prevention of an injury is defined here as all the measures undertaken by police, safety inspectorates, emergency medical services and legal procedures to prevent an accident from occurring or, if and when it happens, to repair the victim such that he does not suffer from any fall in his permanent income during the days of total incapacitation due to this accident or in the future. If the victim does suffer from a loss in permanent income, we would regard that as further social loss from the accident.

The cost of preventing an accident is based on a production function of preventing and repairing personal injury. This production function may be described for a given technology and state of law as:

$$A = F(K, L) \tag{4.5}$$

where A is the level of activity to prevent accident and K and L represent capital and labour inputs for such activity. Given the input prices and the state of law and of technology we can assume that activity and cost would be positively related, such that

$$C = C(A) \tag{4.6}$$
$$\text{and} \quad C' > 0$$

This indicates for example, if crash barriers and ambulance vans become dearer and/or if juries, policemen and doctors have a pay rise, the cost of a level of activity to prevent and to repair personal injury from accidents would also increase.

We further assume that a proximate empirical measure of activity A could be formed in the following relation:

$$A = h(p, X, a) \tag{4.7}$$

where p is the proportion of personal injury cases out of potentially dangerous situations. p is therefore the probability of an 'accident' and $(1-p)$ is the probability of not suffering a loss in permanent income due to an accident. We may now rewrite the cost function as follows:

$$C = C(p, X, a) \tag{4.8}$$

where a represents other influences on activity and therefore on cost, such as severity of law and/or implementation rate of certain legal restraints like the 55 m.p.h. speed limit. It may be reasonably assumed that h_p is negative and h_x and h_a are both positive and therefore $C_p < 0$ and C_x and C_a are both positive. This means: (i) an increase in the probability of an accident for given X and a measures a lower level of activity (i.e. $h_p < 0$) to prevent accidents; (ii) an increase in the frequency of potentially dangerous situations (X) for given values of p and a measures a higher level of activity (i.e. $h_x > 0$); (iii) an increase in the severity and/or implementation rate of law for given values of p and x measures a higher level of activity (i.e. $h_a > 0$).

The number of personal injury cases due to accidents may be regarded as a combination of the act of nature, results of accident prevention and the supply of dangerous situations. One who undertakes a dangerous activity may be assumed to be aware of the probable loss to one's permanent income in the event of an accident besides the pain and suffering from the injury. If this loss is f and the probability of suffering from it is p, the expected utility from undertaking a dangerous activity X, yielding an income flow of Y, may be expressed as:

$$E\{U(Y)\} = (1-p) \cdot U(Y) + p \cdot U(Y-f) \qquad (4.9)$$

In this case a rise in p would lead to a fall in $E\{U(Y)\}$ and a rise in f would lead to a fall in $E\{U(Y)\}$. We may, therefore, write the supply of potentially dangerous situations from an individual as a function of p and f and also of the sum of other influences u, such that:

$$X = X(p, f, u)$$
$$X_p < 0 \qquad (4.10)$$
and $$X_f < 0$$

Equation (4.10) would indicate the aggregate behaviour only under some suitable assumptions about the distribution of p, f and u among all the participants in dangerous activities.

While it is reasonably easy to see how p (or, rather $1-p$) may be treated as a policy instrument, the interpretation of f introduces the complexities ensuing from different compensation systems. If accident costs are allowed to lie where they fall then f will represent the total loss of permanent income suffered by the individual. If, however, we have a compensation system then it is possible that f will be redistributed among other individuals and, possibly, other activities. The behavioural implications of this may be traced in equations (4.9) and (4.10) where any change in f affects our supply of potentially dangerous situations, X. Our utility function may be reinterpreted to include the possibility that compensation payments may be funded from within the activity with insurance premiums or taxes related to accident-proneness and it may also be used to generalise the Calabresi proposition that the imposition of accident liability on the general taxpayer will lead to an increase in total accident cost. Thus, if compensation is to be financed by other activities, the reduction in f will lead to an increase in the supply of X (equation 4.10). There may not be any social cost in compensating part of the loss of permanent income from outside the activity through the general taxpayer. That would be a simple transfer payment, increasing the utility of the people receiving it and decreasing the utility of another group of people forced to pay it. Now, a reduction in f would cause a rise in X, so that $p.f.X$, the social cost of accidents due to non-compensation of the loss of permanent income, would change, depending upon the elasticity of the supply of X due to a change in f. But in the case of accident prevention cost (equation 4.8), if compensation is to be financed by other activities, thus reducing f in the process, there will be an unequivocal increase in prevention cost, since a fall in f causes X to rise through the supply of X in equation 4.10 and a rise in X causes a rise in the prevention cost as in equation 4.8.

We may now combine the net damages, prevention costs and the uncompensated loss of permanent income together to form an additive social loss function as follows:

$$L = D(X) + C(p, X) + p.f.X. \qquad (4.11)$$

All these losses are to be interpreted in the ex ante sense and not as a post-accident or post-compensation income loss. Any potentially dangerous activity has all these three different kinds of costs to the individuals and to society.

Like Becker, we treat p (rather than C) and f as the policy variables in the process of (not) preventing accidents and (not) compensating accident victims. We investigate the optimality conditions for these policy instruments. We do not go on to consider how these optimal values of p and f would change due to some parametric changes, because sufficient conditions for an optimisation problem are satisfied only on a further set of restrictive assumptions.[41]

The optimal values of p and f would satisfy the following first-order conditions:

$$\frac{\delta L}{\delta p} = D'X_p + C'X_p + C_p + p.f.X_p + f.X = 0 \qquad (4.12)$$

$$\frac{\delta L}{\delta f} = D'X_f + C'X_f + p.X + p.f.X_f = 0 \qquad (4.13)$$

Assuming X_p and X_f not to be equal to zero we can rewrite the above conditions as follows:

$$D' + C' + \frac{C_p}{X_p} = -f.p\left(1 - \frac{1}{E_p}\right) \qquad (4.14)$$

$$\text{and } D' + C' = -f.p\left(1 - \frac{1}{E_f}\right) \qquad (4.15)$$

$$\text{where } E_p = -\frac{P}{X} \cdot X_p \qquad (4.16)$$

$$\text{and } E_f = -\frac{f}{X} \cdot X_f$$

The left-hand sides of equations (4.14) and (4.15) may be interpreted as the marginal social cost of increasing the numbers of potentially dangerous situations due to a fall in p and a fall in f respectively. If D' is positive the marginal social cost in equation (4.15) is positive, since C' is always positive. If D' is negative, C' must be greater than D' to ensure positive marginal cost in equation (4.15) and C' plus Cp/Xp must be greater than D' in equation (4.14), since both Cp and Xp are negative. Again, since a reduction in p increases the cost of preventing accidents, and since it also increases the supply of potentially dangerous situations, the marginal social cost of increasing X through a reduction in p is greater than the marginal social cost of increasing X through a fall in f. Now, the right-hand sides of equations (4.14) and (4.15) may be interpreted as marginal revenues and assuming the left-hand sides to be positive, the equality of the two sides is ensured in equation (4.14) if $E_p < 1$ and in equation (4.15) if $E_f < 1$.

It has already been noted that the left-hand side of equation (4.14) is greater than the same in equation (4.15). To maintain a similar relation on the right-hand side we must have $E_p < E_f$. This condition implies that the participants in potentially dangerous activities are, on balance, risk-averse.[42] The economic policy implication is that more than the expected income has to be offered to attract labour to riskier working conditions. It has also been shown above that under certain assumptions both E_f and E_p are less than unity. These optimality conditions may be compared with the actual performance of different industries if the relevant information is available and if one considers the assumption of positive marginal cost to be plausible. Accordingly, a suitable reallocation of resources may be recommended with regard to (non)prevention and (non)compensation of accidents if the optimal magnitudes are not observed.

4.2.2 *An empirical test*

A possible test of the present model comes from the conclusion that at the optimal point $E_p < E_f$. This implies that the participants in the potentially risky activities are risk-averse. To put it differently, there ought to be a wage premium in risky jobs compared to relatively riskless

Table 4.1
The rankings of classified industries according to accident rates
(p) and weekly earnings (α), 1969–72

	Industry Groups	1969 p	1969 α	1970 p	1970 α	1971 p	1971 α	1972 p	1972 α
III	Food, drink and tobacco	5	13	10	10	7	8	8	8
IV	Coal and petroleum products	13	5	10	3	13	3	14	3
V	Chemical and allied industries	9	7	8	6	12	5	9	6
VI	Metal Manufacture	1	3	1	4	1	7	1	4
VII	Mechanical Engineering	8	6	5	9	6	12	7	11
VIII	Instrument Engineering	17	14	15	14	17	15	17	13
IX	Electrical Engineering	16	11	16	12	16	10	16	12
X	Shipbuilding and marine Engineering	3	4	2	5	3	4	2	10
XI	Vehicles	10	2	13	2	10	2	13	1
XII	Metal goods not elsewhere specified	7	9	7	11	8	14	6	15
XIII	Textiles	14	16	14	16	11	16	11	16
XIV	Leather, leather goods and fur	14	18	17	17	15	17	15	18
XV	Clothing and footwear	18	17	18	18	18	18	18	17
XVI	Bricks, pottery, glass, cement etc.	5	10	3	7	2	6	2	5
XVII	Timber, furniture etc.	2	15	6	15	4	13	4	14
XVIII	Paper, printing and publishing	11	1	9	1	13	1	12	2
XIX	Other manufacturing industries	12	8	12	8	9	9	10	9
XX	Construction	4	12	4	13	5	11	5	7
Rank correlation r			·34		·48		·31		·25
Standardised rank correlation: $r/\sigma r$			1·4		2·0		1·3		1·0

ones. A possible test of this hypothesis would be to compare the p-values for different industries with the corresponding wage rates or earnings with the expectations of a positive relationship between the two variables. This may be done with the help of rank correlation, in the absence of a full-fledged model for wage determination as in the case of our present model.

We present in Table 4.1 the eighteen industry groups and their rankings according to p (accident rates) and α (weekly earnings). The industry groups are taken from the Standard Industrial Classification (1968). The data[43] in Table 4.1 are consistent (at 95 per cent significance level) with this hypothesis only for 1970 whereas for 1969, 1971 and 1972 they are not. This may be explained by the fact that other influences on the weekly earnings like the demand for labour, market structure in the supply of labour, the limitations on the mobility of labour between different industries, are ignored in the present specification of the hypothesis. An extension of the present model on these lines is needed before earnings and accident rates can be successfully compared for the different industries.

4.3 Conclusion

In this chapter we have introduced the notion of an optimal accident policy. We have discussed in both general and specific terms the formulation of a socially optimal level of accidents. We began with an extremely individualistic approach and followed the usual process of identifying the sort of externality situations that have led to theoretically based arguments for collective as opposed to individual decision-making. We have treated the problems of information, uncertainty and justice as separate issues in order to highlight the particular issues raised by these problems in a social policy for accidents. Since the policy implications of the strict Paretian approach were adjudged to be extremely limited, we adopted a more aggregative approach based on the concept of the social welfare function. In the second part of the chapter, we proposed a specific loss minimisation function and developed a model of accident policy. We also tested a *behavioural* implication of our model.

In the next three chapters we aim to expand and build on some of the concepts introduced in this chapter. In general, we feel that theoretical approaches to policy formation must be supplemented by detailed empirical work before strong recommendation can be made. It is suggested that the ideas in this chapter form a framework for the more operational studies.

Notes

1 Jeffrey O'Connell, *The Injury Industry and the remedy of no-fault insurance,* Illinois U.P., Urbana 1972.
2 G. Tullock, 'The Charity of the Uncharitable', *Western Economic Journal,* vol. 8, 1970, where Tullock questions the motivation behind many calls for more redistribution through governmental intervention.
3 There are many excellent legal textbooks on the law of torts. See e.g. Harry Street, *The Law of Torts* (5th ed.), Butterworth, London 1972.
4 This criticism is well made by G. Calabresi in his well-known book, *The Costs of Accidents: A Legal and Economic Analysis,* Yale University Press, New Haven 1970.
5 A.K. Sen, *Collective Choice and Social Welfare,* Holden-Day, San Francisco 1970.
6 J.M. Buchanan, *Cost and Choice: an inquiry in economic theory,* Markham, Chicago 1969.
7 J.M. Buchanan, ibid.
8 G. Calabresi, op. cit., p. 18.
9 J.E. Meade, *The theory of economic externalities: the control of the environmental pollution and similar social costs,* Sithoff, Leiden 1973, p. 15.
10 J.M. Buchanan, and W.C. Stubblebine, 'Externality', *Economica,* vol. 29, 1962.
11 R. Coase, 'The Problem of Social Cost', *Journal of Law and Economics,* vol. 3, 1960.
12 A.C. Pigou, *The Economics of Welfare,* (4th ed.), Macmillan, London 1932.
13 J.P. Brown, 'Towards an Economic Theory of Liability', *Journal of Legal Studies,* vol. 1, 1973.
14 J.P. Brown, ibid.
15 R. Turvey, 'On Divergences Between Social Cost and Private Cost', *Economica,* vol. XXX, 1963, pp. 309–13.
16 O.E. Williamson, D.G. Olson and A. Ralston, 'Externalities, insurance and disability analysis', *Economica,* August 1967.
17 P. Burrows, 'On External Cost and the Visible Arm of the Law', *Oxford Economic Papers,* vol. 22, 1970.
18 O.E. Williamson et al., op. cit.
19 R.A. Posner, 'A Theory of Negligence', *Journal of Legal Studies,*

vol. 1, 1972.

20 P. Burrows, op. cit.

21 This diagram is taken from the article by H. Shibata, 'A Bargaining Model of the Pure Theory of Public Expenditure', *Journal of Political Economy*, vol. 79, 1971.

22 J.M. Buchanan and G. Tullock, *Calculus of Consent*, Ann Arbor, Michigan 1962.

23 J. Rawls, *A Theory of Justice*, Clarendon Press, Oxford 1972.

24 A.K. Sen, op. cit.

25 J.M. Buchanan, 'The relevance of Pareto optimality', *Journal of Conflict Resolution*, vol. 6, 1962, pp. 341–54.

26 G. Tullock, *The Logic of the Law*, Basic Books, New York 1971.

27 J. Hirschleifer, 'Where are we now in the Economics of Information?' *American Economic Review*, vol. 63, 1973.

28 V. Goldberg, 'The Economics of Product Safety and Imperfect Information', *The Bell Journal of Economics and Management Science*, vol. 5, no. 2, Autumn 1974.

29 W. Oi (reply to Goldberg), 'The economics of product safety: a rejoinder', *The Bell Journal of Economics and Management Science*, vol. 5, no. 2, Autumn 1974.

30 H.H. Demsetz, 'Some Aspects of Property Rights' *Journal of Law and Economics*, vol. 61, 1966.

31 This term was criticised by Professor R.A. Posner who suggests that the 'old' law and economics were mainly concerned with anti-trust legislation.

32 J.M. Buchanan, 'Cost and Choice', op. cit.

33 R.N. McKean, 'Products Liability: Implications of Some Changing Property Rights', *Quarterly Journal of Economics*, vol. 84, 1970.

34 G.S. Becker, 'Crime and Punishment: An Economic Approach', *Journal of Political Economy*, vol. 76, no. 2, 1968.

35 J.P. Brown, op. cit.

36 G. Calabresi, op. cit., pp. 73–5.

37 P.A. Diamond, 'Accident Law and Resource Allocation', *Bell Journal of Economics and Management Science*, vol. 5, no. 2, Autumn 1974.

38 This is logically equivalent to welfare maximisation. It is much more intuitively satisfactory to specify a loss function in the context of accident policy.

39 D. Ghosh, 'An Analysis of Social Costs from Accidental Personal Injuries', Discussion Paper no. 24 in *Discussion Papers in Industrial Economics*, Department of Industrial Economics, University of

Nottingham, April 1975. The model was originally worked by G.S. Becker, op. cit., in the context of 'Crime and Punishment', but the present adaption of the model could be more suitable for accident analysis than it has been for crime. For discussion of the inadequacies of Becker's Model see J.M. Heineke, 'A note on modeling the criminal choice problem', *Journal of Economic Theory*, vol. 10, 1975.

40 In the lawyers' analysis of accident costs pain and suffering constitute the main source of controversy and this has been at the root of indeterminacy, misuse and even abuse of the common law compensation system. J. O'Connell discusses this in the context of US Auto-accidents in his book, *The Injury Industry*. O'Connell's recommendation of No-fault Insurance excludes payments for pain and suffering because of all the delays and difficulties that emanate from them. But pain and suffering remain an important part of the total accident costs, even though it may cause difficulties for the legal procedures to quantify them.

41 See Becker (op. cit.), Mathematical Appendix. In our case, we further need the following conditions:

(i) $D'' + C'' + C_{pp} \dfrac{1}{\frac{x^2}{p}} + f(1 - \dfrac{1}{E_p}) \dfrac{1}{X_p} > C_p \dfrac{1}{X_p} \dfrac{\delta^2 p}{\delta X \delta P}$

(ii) h_{pp} and C_{pp} are both positive.

42 For the proof of this proposition, see Becker (op. cit.) footnote 20.

43 The data for p are available in the annual issues of *British Labour Statistics* and in *Annual Reports of HM Chief Inspector of Factories*. Because of data limitation eighteen industry groups, group III to group XX, are used in the empirical tests. For data on weekly earnings, we use the 1972 issue of *British Labour Statistics*, Table 22. Only October figures are available for all our industry groups for the four years under consideration. For earlier years, the industry classification is different.

5 Optimal speed on the motorway and some shadow prices

5.1 Introduction

In chapter 3 we developed and tested a macro-theory of accident causation. In chapter 4 we presented a general economic approach to accident analysis and policy formulation. Our aim in this chapter is to integrate these two aspects of our research by using both the technical relationships and our general economic model and applying them to a specific policy problem facing highway authorities i.e. what is the socially optimal average speed on a particular class of road?

In order to attempt to answer this question we have developed a formal economic model from which we have derived a formula for optimal average speed. To give our study an empirical dimension we have inserted exogenous values for time, accident casualties and fuel and have used the speed—casualty relationship estimated in chapter 3. This part of our study could be regarded as an example of an application of cost-benefit analysis to the accident problem. In the second part of the chapter we have re-arranged the terms in our economic model in order to solve the 'dual' of the primal problem. In other words, by assuming that the actual average speed is the optimal speed, we have been able to find values or 'shadow prices' for time and life and also of fuel for a particular empirical period.

5.2 Optimal speed: the theoretical background

In this section we aim to tie in our model for optimal speed with a general approach outlined in the previous chapter. There, we used a very general aggregative social loss minimisation objective function. Here, we use a loss minimisation function with the specific purpose of deriving an optimal average speed for a particular class of road. In general the net social loss L may be described as follows:

$$L = f(V, X, g, T)$$

where V = volume of traffic on the road network per time period (in vehicle miles)
X = number of accident casualties of all types (injuries and fatalities)
g = fuel consumed by the traffic per time period
T = time taken by the above volume of traffic.

We can make this functional relationship more specific by introducing the concept of average speed and showing how it links the variables. It is logically obvious that T and V are related by average speed (S) i.e. $T = \frac{V}{S}$. Furthermore, on the basis of our own experiments in chapter 3 and from independent studies[1] we are also able to specify how X and g are related to speed. We illustrate these relationships in Figure 5.1 assuming an exogenously determined volume of traffic V.

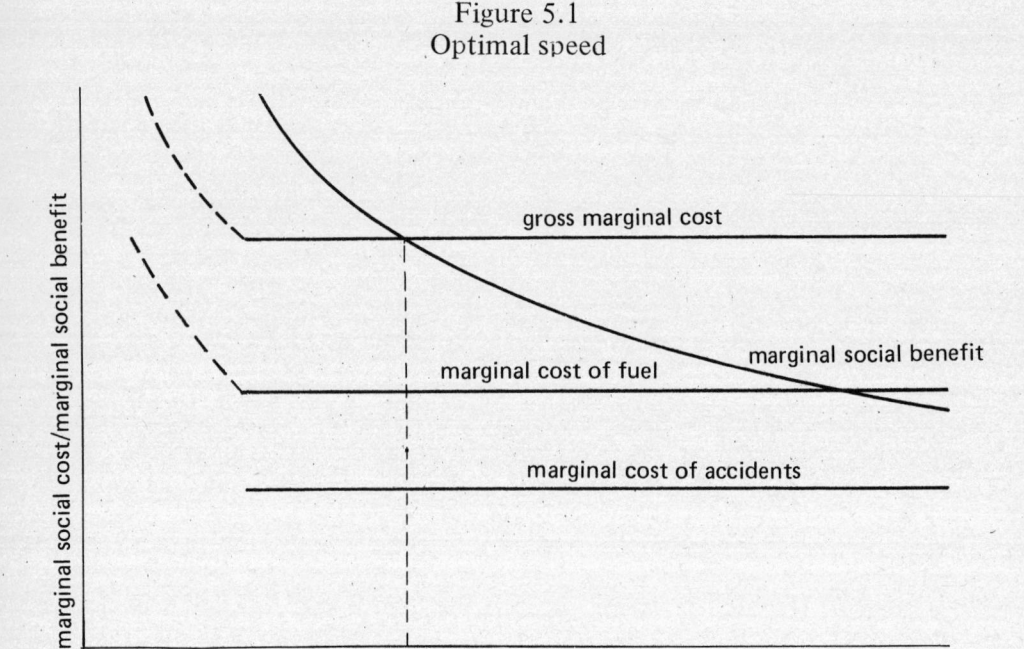

Figure 5.1
Optimal speed

The diagram illustrates the trade-off between the increase in accident costs and fuel consumption and the time saved as speed is increased. Since we have drawn our curves in marginal terms we were able to identify an optimal speed S^* where gross marginal social cost equals gross marginal social benefit which is the condition for a welfare maximum, or, in our particular case, loss minimisation. Let us now develop[2] our approach in a more rigorous manner.

5.3 The model

The marginal social benefit of average traffic speed (S) can be described for a certain exogenously determined volume of traffic during a period. Let this be $\bar{V}$ miles for a month. It would take time T to travel $\bar{V}$ at average speed S, so that we have:

$$\bar{V} = S \cdot T \tag{5.1}$$

or

$$T = \frac{\bar{V}}{S} \tag{5.2}$$

If we now increase speed marginally we may know how much less time it would take to travel $\bar{V}$, the negative of the resulting expression being the amount of time saved.
Therefore:

$$\frac{dT}{dS} = \frac{-\bar{V}}{S^2} \tag{5.3}$$

and gross marginal benefit ($B.p$) of average speed would be:

$$B.p = \frac{-dT}{dS} \cdot p = \frac{\bar{V}}{S^2} \cdot p \tag{5.4}$$

where p is the value of a unit of time saved.

Equation (5.4) indicates the gross marginal benefit of average traffic speed.[3] It should now be corrected for the extra fuel consumption needed for extra speed. One may also include the extra depreciation resulting from higher speed here, but if we ignore this as being relatively insignificant, we may write the following relationship:

$$\frac{\bar{V}}{r} \cdot g(S) \cdot Pg = C \tag{5.5}$$

where,

C = total cost of fuel to travel $\bar{V}$ at average speed, S,
Pg = price of fuel per gallon, (g)

and $g = g(S)$ — the speed–fuel consumption relationship for a given distance r.
The marginal fuel cost of speed from the above impression would be:

$$\frac{dC}{dS} = \frac{\bar{V}}{r} \cdot Pg \cdot \frac{dg}{dS} \tag{5.6}$$

Therefore, net marginal social benefit of speed is now:

$$B.p. \quad -\frac{dC}{dS} = \frac{\overline{V}}{S^2} \cdot p - \frac{\overline{V}}{r} \cdot Pg \cdot \frac{dg}{dS} \qquad (5.7)$$

Let us now look at the accident aspect of speed. Here we assume the relationship in chapter 3 between road casualties and some apparently uncontrollable factors like the volume of traffic ($\overline{V}$), weather indices (W_i) and average vehicle speed (S). This relation may be considered as a 'production function' that is expected to shift in a favourable trend in response to technical innovation and resource allocation for accident prevention. We may write this relation as follows:

$$X = F(t, \overline{V}, s, W) \qquad (5.8)$$

where, X = number of casualties
$\overline{V}$ = volume of traffic
s = average speed of traffic
W = weather index
and t = time.

If the technical innovation is assumed to remain neutral, as in chapter 3 above, we may rewrite the equation as follows:

$$X = A(t) \cdot f(\overline{V}, W, s) \qquad (5.9)$$

For a period of time when the above relation may be assumed to remain stable (i.e. for a period of sufficiently short time to ensure that the technological innovation and resource allocation to prevent motorway accidents will have very little effect on the influence of $\overline{V}$, W and s on X in equation (5.8) above), we may assume either a simple linear or a log linear form of the above function. Thus for equation (5.9) we may either have:

$$X = A + \alpha, \overline{V} + \alpha_2 s + \alpha_3 W \qquad (5.10A)$$

or we may use

$$X = A \cdot \overline{V}^{\beta_1} \cdot s^{\beta_2} \cdot W^{\beta_3} \qquad (5.10B)$$

The marginal accident cost of average speed may now be deduced from the above relation, given the cost of casualty per unit has been calculated as p_X:

$$p_X \cdot \frac{\delta X}{\delta s} = p_X \cdot \alpha_2 \qquad (5.11A)$$

or alternatively:

$$p_x \cdot \beta_2 \cdot A \cdot \bar{V}^{\beta_1} \cdot s^{\beta_2 - 1} \cdot W^{\beta_3} \qquad (5.11B)$$

At the optimal average speed, net marginal benefit of speed must be equal to the marginal cost of speed described above. Therefore at the optimum s, we have:

$$\frac{\bar{V}}{s^2} \cdot p - \frac{\bar{V}}{r} \cdot pg \cdot \frac{dg}{ds} = p_x \cdot \frac{\delta X}{\delta s} \qquad (5.12)$$

or

$$\bar{V} \cdot p = \left(\frac{\bar{V}}{r} \cdot p_g \cdot \frac{dg}{ds} + p_x \cdot \frac{\delta X}{\delta s} \right) \cdot s^2$$

or

$$s = \pm \left(\frac{\bar{V} \cdot p}{\frac{\bar{V}}{r} \cdot p_g \cdot \frac{dg}{ds} + p_x \cdot \frac{\delta X}{\delta s}} \right)^{1/2} \qquad (5.13)$$

If we now assume a linear equation for $g = g(s)$ above, as suggested by the TRRL tests at speeds above forty m.p.h. we may use a constant for $\frac{dg}{ds}$.

Optimal average speed[4] may now be written in two alternative forms:

(a)

$$s = \left(\frac{\bar{V} \cdot p}{\frac{\bar{V} \cdot p_g \cdot \gamma}{r} + p_x \cdot \alpha_2} \right)^{1/2} \qquad (5.14)$$

where α_2 is to be estimated from equation (5.10A); or the solution for the equation for s:

(b)

$$\bar{V}p - \frac{\bar{V}}{r} \gamma \cdot p_g \cdot s^2 - p_x \cdot A \cdot \beta_2 \cdot \bar{V}^1 \cdot s^{\beta_2 + 1} \cdot W^{\beta_3} = 0 \qquad (5.15)$$

where the indices β_1, β_2 and β_3 should be known beforehand from an estimation of equation (5.10B). In what follows it will be more convenient to use equation (5.14) rather than equation (5.15).[5]

Let us now investigate the implications of changing the values of time, of casualties and petrol. In Figure 5.2 we present a slightly different version of Figure 5.1. In the marginal benefit curve the costs of fuel have been netted out, while the marginal cost curve now includes only accident costs. costs. The marginal benefit from traffic speed, as described in equation (5.7) above, falls as speed is increased while the marginal cost in equation (5.11A) remains constant. As before, the interaction of these two curves

Figure 5.2
Change in the optimal speed

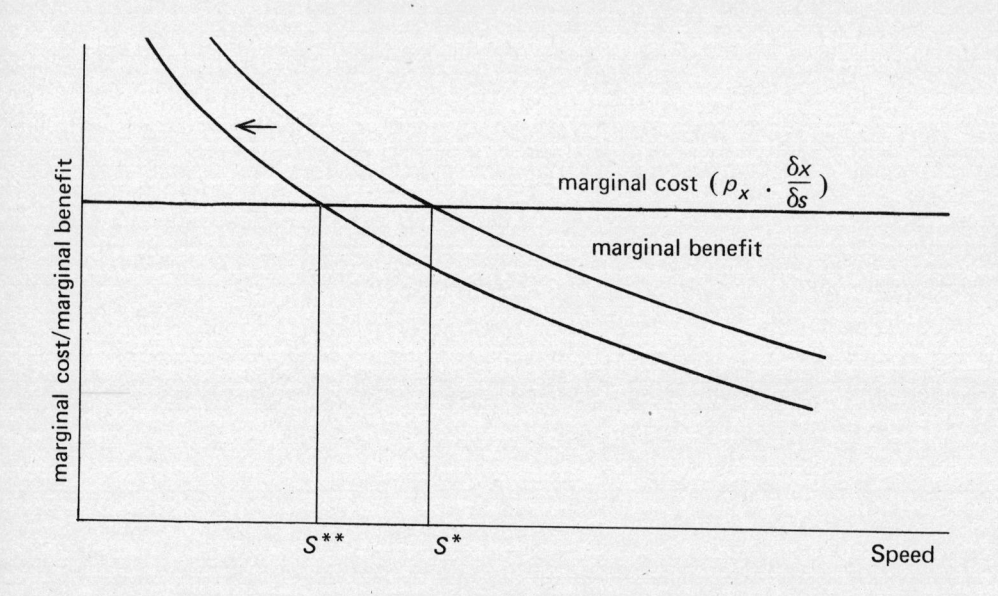

marginal cost $(p_x \cdot \frac{\delta x}{\delta s})$

marginal benefit

S^{**} S^* Speed

determines the optimal traffic speed at S^*. This value of S^* could change if there are changes in the values of the exogenous variables such as $\bar{V}, p_g$ and valuations of time p and casualty p_x. At a certain pair of values for $\bar{V}, p_g$ it is possible to calculate the optimal speed S^* for given values of p and p_x (valuations of time and casualty, respectively) and S^* would automatically change if these valuations are altered. We conduct one such exercise in section 5.5. But a change in p_g, the petrol price, is likely to induce a change in the amount of motoring, possibly along a downward sloping demand curve. It may also lead to a change in the traffic speed as motorists reduce their petrol consumption in covering the same distance. Both these responses could be ignored in our model above because p_g is not allowed to vary for a particular period of time. If we now relax this restriction we can investigate the effect of a change in petrol price (p_g) on the optimal traffic speed (S^*). We can do this in two stages. First we assume that the effect of a change in p_g is only on $\bar{V}$ and not on S and we find that we need to know to sign a corresponding change in S^*. Next we find what we need to know to sign a corresponding change in S^*. Next we find out, if we assume a change in p_g to affect both V and S, what we must know before we can sign the corresponding change in S^*. In Figure 5.2 we illustrate the first case.

A rise in p_g would cause a shift in the marginal benefit curve without affecting the marginal cost curve. The marginal benefit curve would unambiguously shift to the left if we have:

$$\frac{V_{p_g}}{S^2} \cdot p - \frac{V_{p_g}}{r} \cdot p_g \frac{dg}{ds} - \frac{V}{r} \cdot \frac{dg}{ds} < 0 \qquad (5.16)$$

The above inequality involves some marginal changes, one of which we have mentioned above. It is the negative slope of the demand for motoring curve which may be described as follows:

$$V = V(p_g, \text{other variables}) \qquad (5.17)$$
$$\text{and } V_{p_g} < 0$$

When we use the inequality in (5.17) along with our earlier assumptions we find that an unambiguous downward shift of the marginal benefit curve in Figure 5.2 and therefore a fall in S^* would require

$$\frac{V_{p_g}}{S^2} \cdot p + \frac{V}{r} \cdot \frac{dg}{ds} > \frac{V_{p_g}}{r} \cdot p_g \cdot \frac{dg}{ds} \qquad (5.18)$$

The second case of p_g affecting both V and S requires a further relation:

$$S = S(p_g, \text{other variables})$$
$$\text{and} \qquad S_{p_g} < 0 \qquad (5.19)$$

A rise in p_g in this case would cause a downward shift in the marginal cost curve if

$$p_x \cdot \frac{\delta^2 X}{\delta s^2} \cdot \frac{\delta s}{\delta p_g} < 0 \qquad (5.20)$$

But the corresponding change in marginal benefit curve could be downward only if:

$$\frac{S^2 \cdot V_{p_g} - 2 \cdot V \cdot S \cdot S_{p_g}}{S^4} \cdot p - \frac{V}{r} \cdot \frac{dg}{ds} - p_g \cdot \frac{dg}{ds} \cdot \frac{V_{p_g}}{r}$$

$$- \frac{V}{r} \cdot p_g \cdot \frac{d^2 g}{ds^2} ds < 0 \qquad (5.21)$$

The second term in the inequality (5.21) is negative and the third term is positive. The first term is ambiguous if we are ignorant about the relative magnitudes of the terms in the numerator. For a certain period in some country or region, if we assume it to be positive, we can rewrite the inequality in (5.21) as follows: assuming $\frac{d^2 g}{ds^2}$ to be zero:

Figure 5.3
Change in optimal speed due to a rise in petrol price

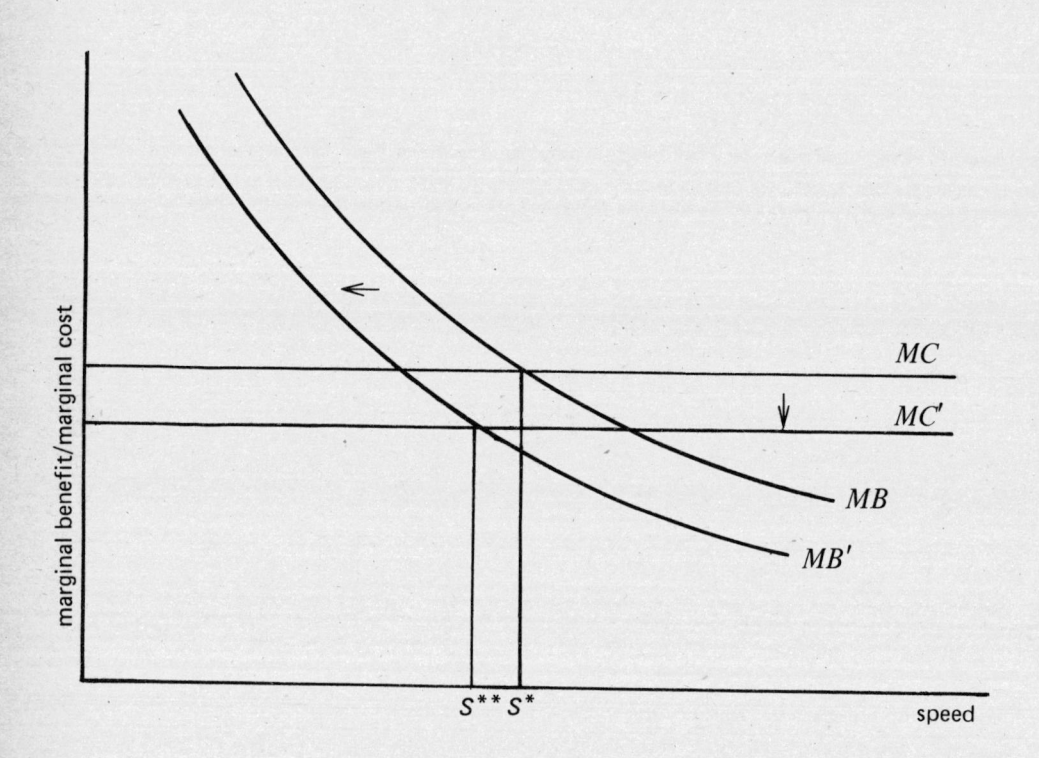

$$\frac{S^2 \cdot V_{p_g} - 2 \cdot V \cdot S \cdot S_{p_g}}{S^4} \cdot p + p_g \cdot \frac{dg}{ds} \cdot \frac{V_{p_g}}{r} < \frac{V}{r} \cdot \frac{dg}{ds} \qquad (5.22)$$

A rise in p_g could cause a downward shift in the marginal cost curve for speed, under the condition in inequality (5.20). The marginal benefit curve would also shift to the left due to an increase in p_g, under the condition formalised in inequality (5.22).

But it should be noted that a rise in petrol price could shift both the marginal benefit/cost curves for speed either way or it may not shift them at all. Optimal speed would unambiguously increase or unambiguously decrease for some combinations of the above shifts in marginal benefit/cost of speed, but for some other cases its direction of change remains ambiguous. In such cases the change depends on the relative

Table 5.1
Changes in the optimal speed due to an increase in petrol price

Marginal benefit	Marginal cost	Optimal speed
Rise	Rise	Ambiguous
Rise	Fall	Increase
Fall	Rise	Decrease
Fall	Fall	Ambiguous
Same	Rise	Decrease
Same	Fall	Increase
Rise	Same	Increase
Fall	Same	Decrease

magnitudes of the various kinds of responses mentioned above. We present below all the possible combinations of the shifts in the marginal benefit/cost curves of speed and the subsequent change in the optimal speed.

We should mention here that the shifts in the marginal benefit/cost of speed refer to the rise in petrol price only, when all the other variables affecting the choice of traffic volume and traffic speed are assumed to remain unchanged. But such changes are occurring all the time and the optimal speed may also vary accordingly even when petrol price remains unchanged.

In this section we have presented a model for the optimal average traffic speed on the basis of some given valuations of time and casualty and also for a particular volume of traffic during a period of time when the price of petrol remains unchanged. This optimal speed would have a different value if we change the valuations of time and casualty. We have also shown that at the same level of these valuations, if we change the petrol price, both the desired volume of traffic and the desired average speed of travel may change to alter the optimal average speed. We have derived expressions which indicate what we need to know in order to predict how the optimal speed will change with changes in the price of petrol.

We are now in a position to apply our model to a particular road network in a specified time period. However, let us first consider some of the theoretical and practical problems raised by the need to insert numbers for p_g, p_x and p.

5.4 The valuation problem

The idea of consciously putting a monetary value on a human life strikes many as being morally and emotionally abhorrent. Yet the constant theme of our approach is that, firstly, the optimal level of accidents for society is unlikely to be zero and that, secondly, since individuals can be observed to be voluntarily risking life and limb in order to attain other goals they do put an implicit value on changes in risk levels. This last point needs to be stressed since it is very rare indeed for an individual to voluntarily accept certain death and, when he does, it is usually for strictly non-economic notives.[6]

The clear difference between the two situations is that while individuals may be prepared to accept a sum of money in exchange for a higher risk level, there is probably no sum large enough to compensate him for certain death.[7] A further related observation is that a linear relationship between the probability of a person being killed and the sum he would be prepared to accept for an increase in risk is highly unlikely. As E. J. Mishan puts it: 'The implied assumption of linearity which has it that a man who accepts $100,000 for an assignment offering him a four-to-one chance of survival will agree to go to certain death for $500,000 is implausible, to say the least.'

As Mishan shows, it is conceptually possible to calculate the change in the probability of a death occurring for a particular project appraisal; it is not necessary therefore to place a value on an average life.

While most academic economists are now agreed on the theoretical desiderata for the evaluation of life, in practice, it has proved extremely difficult to produce any operational numbers. The current consensus in the literature seems to be that whatever misgivings economists generally have about the method, a questionnaire approach is the only way by which individual valuations can be obtained. While attempts have been made to develop a suitable questionnaire, so far, widely varying figures have been published. Our model generates changes in the aggregate number of casualties which can only be valued by having a 'price' for a fatality and the various classes of injury.[8] For both the above reasons we were forced to use the figures used by the Department of the Environment in its own cost-benefit studies. As we are not merely concerned with fatalities and our model specifies a single value p_x, we have had to meet this problem by developing the concept of a 'unit' of accident which we will explain in the next section.

The idea of valuing time is less likely to involve the moral and emotional issues raised by the valuation of life. Once again, we may observe that individuals place a value on time in the sense that they are prepared to trade other goods in order to attain time savings.[9] Since time savings constitute such an important aspect of transportation studies there is considerable literature on the theoretical and practical problems of evaluating time savings.[10] While it is theoretically plausible and operationally easy to measure the marginal productivity of working-time by looking at hourly wage rates and make assumptions about the labour market, the valuation of time, particularly leisure time, in terms of our Paretian methodology is far more difficult. Most cost-benefit analysts differentiate between various 'types' of time such as commuting time, leisure time and work time and would not consider the single hourly figures chosen in our model to be appropriate to the complexity of the problem. Our third problem is presented by the need to estimate the value of fuel saved by reductions in speed. The practical and theoretical difficulties are, of course, considerably easier than those posed by time and life since petrol is traded in a well established market. In most countries, however, the pump price of fuel includes a very high percentage of excise tax. In the UK, for example, some variable percentage of the price of a gallon of petrol is accounted for by excise and value added tax. In addition, the world price of oil is at present set by an extremely effective international monopoly (OPEC) which further distorts the extent to which pump prices represent real resource costs. We may safely assume that in consumer countries, at least, the import price represents a very real resource cost however highly centralised world oil production is. The treatment of petrol taxes is more problematic.

The cost-benefit literature is divided on the issue of indirect taxes. R. Layard[11] suggests that a correction for indirect taxes is required only if the tax is seen purely as a revenue raiser. Thus: 'where there is a rationale, such as the correction of external diseconomies (via a fuel tax), the discouragement of "merit loads" (like smoking) or the redistribution of income, no adjustment may be called for'. It is probable that there are significant external diseconomies in highway transportation. In spite of this, the convention in the UK studies of road projects is to exclude petrol taxes. As Millward puts it: 'The argument [for excluding petrol tax] is that the value of making car journeys — looking at the fuel item only — is equal to the price of petrol net of tax since such a figure represents the cost of producing petrol (or rather, refining, in the UK environment).'[12] It should be evident that even this brief review of the valuation problems gives some indication of the complexities of the issues involved. It will also be evident that we have introduced many simplifications in the application of our model.

5.5 An application of the model

We now apply our model to recent British experience on the motorways. The advantage of using the motorways is that they are relatively homogeneous in technical characteristics in contrast to the heterogeneity of other rural and urban roads. However, it can be seen in the historical evidence of the imposition of speed limits and also on the basis of international experience, that the optimisation process described in 5.3 is perfectly general to all types of road in different countries. In an attempt to meet the difficulties of specifying a single price for time we present a range of values (see Table 5.2). The highest value used is £1 an hour. This is close to the hourly wage rate during August 1973. In our case the time saved is calculated for a vehicle, whereby average time saved may accrue to more than one person.

The conceptual problems of valuing life and limb have already been discussed. Our requirement is to derive some valuation of a 'unit' of accident in order to estimate the aggregate social cost of accidents for a certain period. Despite their theoretical shortcomings the most widely used empirical estimates of different types of casualties, viz. fatalities, serious and slight injuries, are to be found in R. F. F. Dawson's work.[13] We used the 1973 estimates of his valuation.

For fatalities, Dawson includes future loss of output less future consumption, funeral and ambulance cost and some 'non-resource costs' of '... suffering and bereavement..' For other kinds of casualties these 'subjective' costs are reckoned to be much less.

There is some problem in classifying casualties into the various categories since many discrepancies between the police and hospital records have been recorded.[14] Even the definition of a fatality has not been agreed upon on an international basis. With these problems in mind we have calculated a composite accident unit which is derived from the weighted sum of the TRRL valuations. The weights for fatalities, serious and slight injuries were calculated from the average monthly casualty of each type during the period January 1972 to March 1974. These weights are 4·33 per cent, 26·5 per cent and 69·17 per cent respectively. The weights are then multiplied by the TRRL valuation of motorway accidents of each type, including non-human damages. The sum of these weighted valuations is the value of the unit of casualty (p_x in equation (5.11)) and comes out as £2,445.

The relation between rate of petrol consumption and speed has been worked out by the Transport and Road Research Laboratory.[15] From this experiment the extra petrol required for an extra mile of speed (m.p.h.) turns out to be ·052 gallons (in equation (5.14)) for a distance of 100 miles (r in equation (5.5)) on the motorways between speeds 40 m.p.h. to 70 m.p.h. As can be seen in Figure 5.4, the relation between fuel consumption and observed average speed is approximately U-shaped, though after 40–42 m.p.h. this relation also becomes linear. Once we have calculated $\frac{dC}{ds}$ in equation (5.6) from other information on petrol price and traffic volume, we may easily calculate the net marginal social benefit of speed from equation (5.7). The production function relation of equation (5.8) between casualties and volume of traffic, corrected for density, speed and weather conditions, has been worked out already for British motorways, using monthly figures for the period January 1972 to March 1974. This period is not lengthened any further because possible change in $A(t)$ during a longer period may not comply with the assumption of a non-shifting functional relationship. Certain weather conditions like fog, snow, rainfall are assumed to be random as well as other factors, such as mechanical failures, inexperienced and/or tired drivers. The total impact of these random variables is expected to follow a normal distribution with zero mean and finite variance, so that we may be able to fit a multiple regression for the equations (5.10A) or (5.10B). The units used for our estimates are:

$\overline{V}$ = million vehicle miles per month for a mile of motorway
s = average motorway speed (m.p.h.) for a month
W = hours of daily average sunshine for a month.

Our estimates for the two equations (5.10A) and (5.10B) are as follows:

$$X = -1169 \cdot 70 + 746 \cdot 66 \overline{V} + 18 \cdot 49 s - 24 \cdot 6 W$$
$$(5 \cdot 16) \quad (6 \cdot 34) \quad (4 \cdot 46) \quad (2 \cdot 69) \quad (5.10\text{A}')$$

$$R^2 = \cdot 819; \ \overline{R}^2 = \cdot 795; \ D.W = 2 \cdot 08; \ F = 27 \cdot 15$$

$$\log X = -5 \cdot 41 + 1 \cdot 62 \log \overline{V} + 2 \cdot 96 \log s - 0 \cdot 2 \log W$$
$$(2 \cdot 38) \quad (6 \cdot 46) \quad (5 \cdot 3) \quad (2 \cdot 73)$$

$$R^2 = \cdot 853; \ \overline{R}^2 = \cdot 834; \ D.W. = 1 \cdot 58; \ F = 34 \cdot 75 \quad (5.10\text{B}')$$

The numbers within brackets are the corresponding t-values. It seems both the equations are well-determined, with the expected signs for all the coefficients, all of which are statistically significant.

We are now in a position to calculate the optimum average speed from equation (5.14) and (5.15) above. In our calculation we use equation (5.10A') for an estimate of $\frac{\delta X}{\delta s}$ in equation (5.14) because it is almost as well determined as in equation (5.10B'), and also because it involves much

Figure 5.4
Speed and fuel consumption

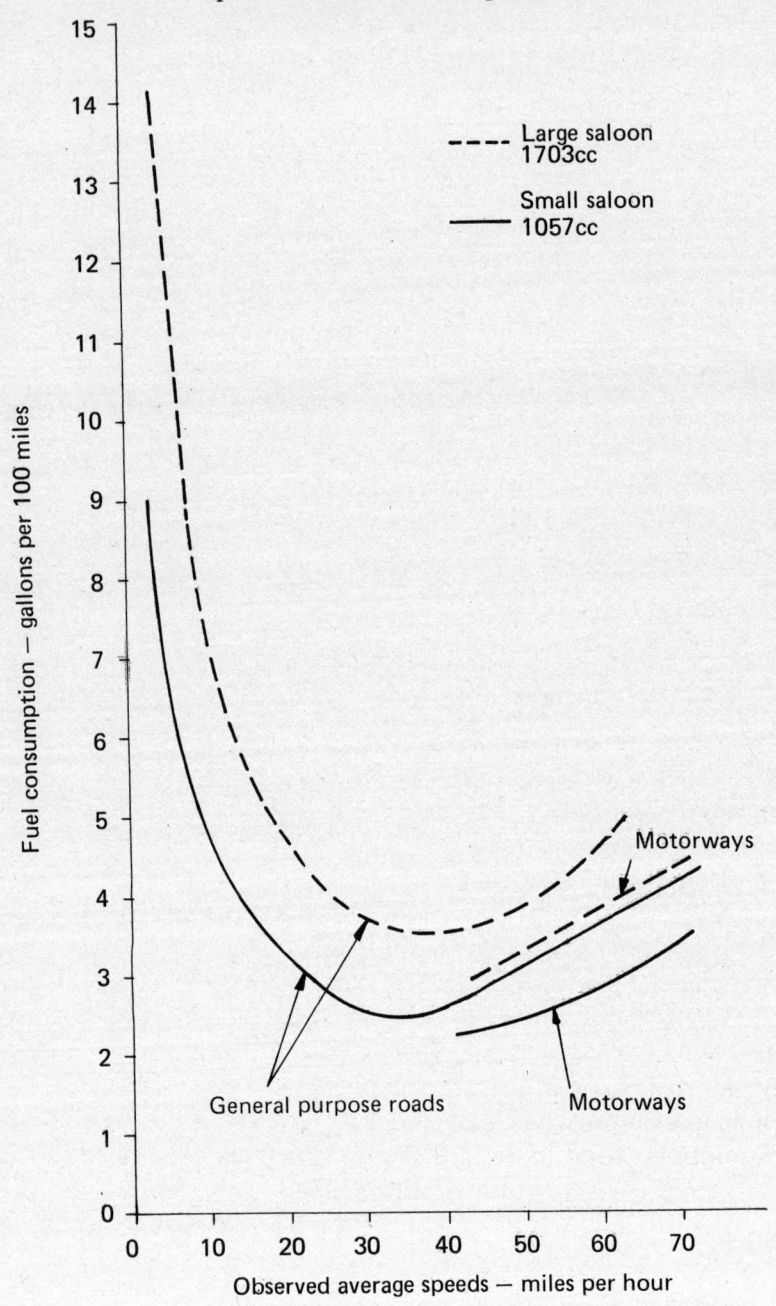

less computation than the other procedure for an estimate of $\frac{\delta X}{\delta S}$ in equation (5.15). It may be noted that in the case of equation (5.15) weather would affect the optimal average speed while in equation (5.10B′) it would not. The effect of weather from equation (5.10B′), however, seems to be numerically insignificant.

Table 5.2
Optimal average speeds (m.p.h.)

Value of a unit of casualty (p_x) \ Value of time per hour (p)	£1·00	£0·50	£0·25
£2,445·34	67·45	47·69	33·72
£4,890·68	62·30	44·05	31·15

The optimal average speed can be calculated for any month during the period January 1972 to March 1974 and, when applied to the volume of traffic for August 1973 (1195 million miles), indicates the above values. They are calculated for different combinations of valuation of time saved in motorway transport, for different valuations of accidents and for the average price of petrol at the time of about 35p per gallon.

It is noticeable that a reduction in the valuation of time and on increase in the valuation of casualty both reduce optimum speed, though it is far more sensitive to changes in the value of time. This is so because value of time is multiplied by the entire time saved, whereas the value of a unit of casualty is applicable to the relatively low number of units in the same equation.

It may be mentioned here that technological innovation and resource allocation in preventing accidents due to speed and reducing the rate of fuel consumption from speed are likely to reduce the values of both $\frac{\delta X}{\delta s}$ and $\frac{dg}{ds}$ so that the values indicated in Table 5.2 would change accordingly, even when the valuations of casualty and time and the price of petrol may be assumed to be unchanged. But a change like $\frac{\delta X}{\delta s}$ or $\frac{dg}{ds}$ may not happen frequently or may not be large within a short time, so that the values of optimal average speed may be stable for some time.

In the introduction we presented our model as an example of a cost-benefit analysis. It may not be clear how this term can be applied since the technique is generally used in evaluating specific projects such as bridge, reservoir and road schemes. In other words, it may not be obvious how our concept of optimal speed can be related to a specific policy measure. If we knew the relationship between average speed and speed limits, and also had some estimate of the extra enforcement costs entailed in a lower speed limit then it is conceptually possible to use our approach to evaluate the costs and benefits of lowering the motorway speed limit. If such an operational cost-benefit analysis was undertaken then there are many ways in which a model could be expanded and made more sophisticated. For example, the composition of the motorway traffic could be studied in order to facilitate a certain amount of disaggregation in the calculation in its present form. However, our model could equally well be applied to study the effects of a deliberate change in the price of fuel through taxation. As recent international experience shows, dramatic rises in petrol prices have been followed by lower speeds, less motoring and lower accident levels. We do feel, however, that our general approach is useful and that it could form the basis of more sophisticated and operational studies on the costs and benefits of changing speed limits. Whether the political will exists to implement these studies and make the trade off process absolutely explicit is quite another matter which we can only touch on in this book (see chapters 4 and 7).

5.6 Some shadow prices

In section 5.5 we used some given values of time and casualty and the contemporary price of petrol in order to calculate the socially optimal speed on the motorways for an exogenously determined volume of traffic over a particular month. In this section we make a different set of assumptions in order to find some implied values for petrol and also for the intangibles of time and life. We therefore do the following experiments:

1 We find out the shadow price of time assuming actual average speed to be the optimal speed, given some valuation of a typical mix of casualties and the price of petrol at the time.
2 We find out the shadow price of a fatal casualty, assuming the actual average speed to be the optimal speed, given some valuation of time and the price of petrol at the time.

3 We find out some implied valuation of petrol, given the TRRL valuations of motorway accidents of different types, their corresponding weights in total casualties and some valuation of time and assuming the actual average speed to be the optimum speed.

All these may be calculated by the appropriate rearrangement of terms in equation (5.14) as above.

In Table 5.3 we present the hypothetical values of time, for two different valuations of a unit of casualty. We note that a 100 per cent change in p_x causes much less change in p. If we regard social valuations of lives and limbs lost in motorway accidents to be correctly measured by the Transport and Road Research Laboratory during 1973, the assumption of optimal behaviour by the motorists with regard to speed would imply a social valuation of time of 76p an hour.

Table 5.3
Valuations of time

p	p_x = £2445·34	p	p_x = £4890·68
Value of an hour saved	£0·760637		£0·892020

Our valuation of a life (motorway fatality) turns out to be £94,000 when value of time is £1·00 an hour, the price of petrol is 35p a gallon and speed is assumed to be optimal at its actual average level of 58·8 m.p.h. If we decrease the valuation of time the implied value of a life becomes zero at 63p an hour and it becomes negative after that. This is understandable. An increase in speed causes some saving in time which, when valued at reduced prices, may not compensate for the extra fuel cost of extra speed for a traffic volume of hundreds of millions of miles, thus resulting in a negative valuation of life.

Finally, even though its price is determined in the market, for the sake of logical completeness, we look into an implied value of petrol.

It may be noted that the implied value of petrol at £1·00 per hour value of time has been nearly 37 per cent higher than its actual price at the time (35p per gallon during August 1973) when the typical casualty cost £2445·34.

Table 5.4
Valuations of petrol

p_x \ p	£1·00	£0·50	£0·25
£2445·34	£0·48	£0·21	£0·07
£4890·68	£0·41	£0·13	Negative

It might be argued that the dual solutions are only of academic interest and that they do not have the potential policy applications of the 'primal' presentation of the model. This argument is not altogether convincing since, as Culyer suggests,[16] one use of the dual process is to derive: 'the implicit values placed on the margin by decision-makers, to make them explicit and then to ask them – the responsible deciders – whether what they are actually doing is what they thought they were doing or what they wanted to do.'

Thus in our case we may derive an implicit value for life and time and consider whether the actual speeds are 'implying' socially acceptable values. We do have the problem that in order to solve for one unknown, we have to use a controversial valuation for one of the intangibles, that is, our solution is heavily dependent on the numbers we choose for life and time.

Our shadow price for life does have pedagogical usefulness since it represents the value implied by the political process put forward by T. C. Schelling[17] and rejected decisively by Mishan as a possible source of valuation of life for use in cost-benefit studies. As Mishan points out:[18] 'Where the outcome of the political debate calls upon the economist to provide a quantitive evaluation of the project under consideration, the economist fails to meet his brief insofar as he abandons the attempt to calculate every aspect of the project by reference to an economic criterion and, instead, attempts to extricate figures from previous political decisions.' This criticism does not fully apply to our shadow prices since it is evident that the actual average speed is arrived at with a mixture of private and collective decisions. Similarly, we cannot attribute a particular implied valuation of life or time solely to a collective decision on speed limits or petrol price.

Notes

1 Department of the Environment, *Getting the best roads for our money: The COBA method of appraisal*, HMSO, 1972.

2 The main part of the present model has been already published: D. Ghosh, D. Lees and W. Seal, 'Optimal motorway speed and some valuations of time and life', *The Manchester School*, June 1975.

3 As most drivers have a pure taste for speed, up to a point, then 'B.p' will tend to underestimate the gross marginal benefit of average speed as described in equation 5.4.

4 The second order condition requires that s in equation 5.14 be positive and not negative.

5 One may solve (5.15) by the use of Maclaurin's Expansion, given the values of the parameters and the exogenous variables.

6 Here we are clearly referring to the sort of narrow, materialistic motivation usually attributed to that mythical monster, Economic Man.

7 E. J. Mishan, 'The Value of Life', *The Journal of Political Economy*, 1971.

8 It should be noted, however, that our model could, in principle, be modified in order to accommodate valuations of changes in the probability of death and injury rather than valuations of lives and various types of injury.

9 G. S. Becker, 'A theory of the allocation of time', *Economic Journal*, September 1965.

10 A. J. Harrison and D. A. Quarmby, 'The value of time', in *Cost Benefit Analysis*, R. Layard (ed.), Penguin, Harmondsworth 1972; N. Lee and M. Q. Dalvi, 'Variations in the Value of Travel Time', *The Manchester School*, September 1969; N. Lee and M. Q. Dalvi, 'Variations in the Value of Travel Time: further analysis', *The Manchester School*, September 1971.

11 R. Layard (ed.), *'Cost Benefit Analysis'*, Penguin, Harmondsworth 1972.

12 R. Millward, *'Public Expenditure Economics'*, McGraw-Hill, London 1971.

13 R. F. F. Dawson, 'Current Costs of Road Accidents in Great Britain', *TRRL Report LR 396*, 1971.

14 J. P. Bull and B. J. Roberts, 'Road Accident Statistics - A Comparison of Police and Hospital Information', *Accident Analysis and Prevention*, vol. 5, 1973.

15 See Department of the Environment, op.cit.

16 A. J. Culyer, *'The Economics of Social Policy'*, Martin Robertson, London 1973.

17 T. C. Schelling, 'The life you save may be your own', in S. B. Chase, (ed.), *Problems in Public Expenditure Analysis,* The Brookings Institution, Washington, DC 1968, pp. 127-76.

18 E. J. Mishan, op.cit.

6 Other accident areas

6.1 Accident classification

In our use of road accident data in chapters 3 and 5, we considered a major category of accidental injury that has an obvious locational frame of reference. It is clear, however, that such a classification does not merely reflect location but, more fundamentally, a social judgement on responsibility. For example, it is evident that whatever system of compensation is practised, almost all countries regard the prevention of road accidents as being the responsibility of central and local government. Although we can observe widespread government intervention in the shape of a plethora of regulations and inspectorates, we cannot be quite as dogmatic about accidents at work. While opinions clearly differ on the desirability or extent of such intervention, it is probably a fact of political life in a pluralistic society that there will be pressures on legislators 'to do something about' industrial accidents, particularly as we are generally faced with a potential conflict situation between management and employees, both of which represent powerful political lobbies.

We may extend this 'societal' explanation of accident classification by considering a further major grouping, accidents in the home. Here again, the important point of the classification is not the locational aspect but the social attitude towards responsibility for accidents and accident prevention. If, for example, an individual trips over the cat and breaks a leg, society may compensate him for loss of earnings and medical costs as part of a social insurance scheme, but it is unlikely to be concerned about the cause of injury. If, however, an individual is injured in a motor accident then both the criminal law and civil law are generally involved. The economist (and the courts) would probably argue that the distinction between the two accidents is that the first accident is purely a personal matter concerning the individual (and, of course, the cat) alone while the road accident resulted in an externality problem.[1] One possible pitfall in this approach is that it involves an implicit value judgement concerning the definition and policy implications of the concept of externality. Furthermore, it is not self evident that there is unanimity on who is responsible either technically or morally for many types of accident. The epidemiologist, for example, is unlikely to dismiss home accidents as casually as we have done, since, from a medical point of view, the concern will be more with the possible statistical significance of a potential health hazard rather than with issues of personal and social responsibility. Thus, while we can be fairly confident that the accident with the cat will not be the subject of public discussion, it is probably more a function of its randomness as an accident situation rather than a reflection of total consensus on the demarcation line between public and private responsibility. If a strong link between cause and effect can be established, as, for example, between smoking and lung cancer, then the pressure builds up to ban or regulate an activity which, in its health hazard aspects at least, cannot be said to generate external effects. Thus, in the UK it has recently been made compulsory for a motor cyclist to wear a crash helmet even though the limitation of physical trauma offered by a crash helmet is clearly confined to the motor cyclist.

Following the well-known dictum 'prevention is better than cure', preventive medicine has become increasingly popular with the medical profession. The debate over safety legislation frequently does not extend beyond purely medical and technical questions, for there has been only sporadic resistance to this process. There are signs, however, of growing resistance to the threat to individual freedom posed by the medical establishment (see I. Illich[2]). At some stage in the not too distant future society must face the moral implications as well as the technical problems of preventive medicine.

From a medical or, more strictly speaking, an epidemiological point of view, there are thousands of different ways of classifying accidents. Thus classification may be based on the location of the accident, the accident 'host' (sex, age of victim), the objects involved in the accident, the time of day, the weather conditions, and so on. Each classification implicitly represents a potential theory of accident causation. The word 'theory' is perhaps misleading since the essence of the epidemiological approach is that the researcher should not allow his a priori expectations about the cause of accidents to result in a failure to discover less obvious but *statistically* significant relationships.

A sophisticated example of the epidemiological approach is provided by the National Electronic Injury Surveillance System (NEISS) as designed for the US Consumer Product Safety Commission. The basic idea of the system is to monitor the frequency of particular types of accidents and injuries on a nationwide basis. Data on the injury and circumstances of the victim are collected by a sample of hospitals. The data are then processed centrally by a computer which presents rank-ordered frequency and relative severity distributions. The main aim of the system is to identify the causes of the home accidents and particularly those related to the use of products. The implications of the process are clear. If it is noted that a particular product has a high accident involvement rate, investigation on the nature of the hazard follows in order to consider whether new regulations are required.

As well as being the subject of a growing body of statutory regulations, product related accidents have generated their own case law. In the next section we will consider the social and legal issues raised in product related accidents using the general economic methodology as outlined in chapter 4.

6.2 Product liability

Product liability is that branch of accident law which deals with the personal injuries occurring in connection with the use of products. While it is clear that the classification of accidents by product gives us a legal toehold into home accidents, product liability cases may subsume accidents in all the traditional accident groupings. For example, although we have suggested that the prevention of road accidents is largely a government responsibility, R. Nader[3] has argued to great effect that many personal injuries on the road are the responsibility of the automobile manufacturer.

Liability rules do not necessarily require a particularly active role from the courts. Indeed, the principle of 'caveat emptor' or 'let the buyer beware' allows accident costs to 'lie where they fall'. This principle reflects a conscious legal decision as much as the more interventionist 'caveat vendor' or 'let the seller beware'. Since it is probable that the implicit liability rule underlying the usual competitive market model is caveat emptor, we should not be surprised if economists have a prejudice against other rights assignments which by definition constitute an erosion of consumer sovereignty.

Disagreement over the correct domain of private decision-making, risk-taking and accident cost bearing against the collective assumption of these responsibilities represents a constant source of controversy in product liability issues. This particular policy chestnut is probably more pertinent in the product liability situation than it is, for example, in road accident policy. Even the most individualistic economist would probably agree to a fair amount of government intervention in road safety given the obvious 'public good' nature of the externality (see chapter 4). With products liability, however, property rights are usually fairly well defined and it is consequently relatively easy to analyse the ways by which different liability arrangements will affect the output and pricing of risky products. Decisions may plausibly be assumed to be made by those 'bread and butter' inhabitants of economic models, utility maximising consumers and profit maximising firms. No unfamiliar models of collective decision-making are required but merely an application of the first law of demand and other mainstream economic topics such as imperfect competition and decision-making under risk.

An excellent example of how standard consumer theory may be applied to the analysis of hazardous products is presented by Professor Walter Y. Oi.[4] Oi assumes that the accident risks are inherent in the product and that different grades reflecting different proportions of faulty (accident causing) units are available. The consumer maximises his expected utility function against a budget constraint in which the prices of the products comprise a 'normal' price for the goods plus expected accident costs. These prices Oi calls the 'full' price of the product. Unlike usual market prices, the full price varies between individuals. Thus, for example, the rich consumer will have higher expected accident costs than a poor consumer. Having derived demand curves for risky products, Oi considers how product bans and charges in legal liability affect market demand and hence aggregate accident costs.

While Oi verifies the intuitively plausible prediction that a ban on the riskier product will reduce accident costs, his model questions the usual assertion that a change from consumer liability to producer liability will also reduce accident costs (see J. M. Buchanan[5] and R. N. McKean[6]). If the producer can practise perfect price discrimination then it will not matter if liability is imposed on the consumer or the producer. Without price discrimination, the producer will charge the same full price to all consumers regardless of individual differences in expected accident costs. The redistributive effects of this rule are clear. The full supply price which includes an average damage cost will favour the richer, high accident cost consumer and harm the poorer, low accident cost consumer. The allocative results are less clear. Buchanan and McKean suggest that the shift to producer liability would discourage the production of riskier products. Oi shows that under certain conditions it is the safer products that are no longer produced with a consequent rise in aggregate accident costs.[7]

While the value of rigorous modelling is illustrated by the derivation of such a non-obvious result, the methodology of an approach which requires particularly unrealistic assumptions in the context of products liability is not without its critics. For example, Goldberg[8] criticises Oi for assuming away the problem of imperfect information which seemingly is at the heart of the whole product liability debate. Oi[9] met this criticism by showing that his model could be extended to include imperfect information and by making the general comment that theoretical models need not be rejected merely because direct policy implications cannot be drawn from them. In a similar vein, R. Dorfman[10] criticises Buchanan and McKean for discussing liability rules in a world of perfect competition when it is obvious that the ability of consumers to distinguish between different producers depends on the existence of some form of product differentiation. It follows that the correct scenario for discussing products liability is imperfect rather than perfect competition. Here again we may accept that while it may be fallacious to draw direct welfare implications from theoretical models, some element of abstraction from reality is a fundamental process in positive economics. In fact, both Dorfman's and Goldberg's criticisms may be avoided if the theoretical analysis is pursued in the cautious manner outlined by McKean (see chapter 4).

While we have already come across the rule that in order to minimise the sum of accident costs and accident prevention costs we should place liability on the cheapest accident avoider, it is not always easy to see where the balance of advantage lies. If we consider, for example, the supply of information, we can see that the producer probably has an advantage in the collation of information about the inherent risks of his product. On the other hand, the consumer is in a far better position to know how he is actually going to use the product. The issue is not much clearer when we look at the problem of supply and dissemination of information in a more general setting.

As we saw in chapter 4, there are three possible policy solutions to the problem of information provision. Firstly, we may allow individuals to gather their own information. This may involve a certain amount of 'learning-by-doing' which, in connection with dangerous products, may be unacceptably costly in the short run. Secondly, we may feel that since information has some characteristics of a public good, the state has some responsibility to collect and disseminate it. Finally, we might consider it is more 'cost effective' to abrogate the usual right of the consumer by regulating the use of certain products and/or shifting the costs of the accidents they cause from the consumer/victim to the producer. Solutions two and three differ from each other in terms of attitudes toward individual competence since the third solution clearly transfers some elements of choice away from the consumer. Calabresi[11] would agrue that this solution may be further subdivided since the regulation of products constrains individual decision-making more than the imposition of liability on the producer. The latter approach is the so-called 'market' approach since although the choice of goods and prices they must pay will be altered by an imposed decision on risk levels and accident costs, individuals are still free to buy the goods. The difference between Buchanan's market solutions and Calabresi's market deterrence serves to illustrate the difference in emphasis on the essential features of market exchange. On the one hand, the pure Paretian approach of Buchanan stresses the subjective nature of costs and how they may only possess normative significance at the precise moment of market exchange (see Buchanan[12]). On the other hand Calabresi clearly feels that accident costs and accident avoidance costs can be objectively determined and that the same third party that determines accident costs can also determine the 'cheapest accident avoider'. Such a divergence of opinion may merely reflect Dorfman's distinction between the role of lawyers who are used to making social decisions and economists whose professional duties do not include making decisions in specific situations.

Calabresi's more general criticism of the economic approach is its attempt to make policy generalisations without considering the particular accident and accident avoiding technology. Paradoxically, his objection to the fault system is that the courts are too concerned with the details of the individual case. Clearly, his aim is to try to steer a path between the extreme ad hocery exhibited by the courts and the ivory tower generalisations of the economist. The means for attaining this objective is an institution which is capable of collating and processing the necessary empirical information on accident technology and also making the necessary value judgements on which is the cheapest class of accident avoider.

This last point illustrates a difference in emphasis between Oi, the pure economist, and Calabresi, the lawyer-turned-economist. In his attempt to derive policy inplications directly from a priori analysis, Oi is implicitly setting up a government versus market choice situation. Calabresi, on the other hand, hints that the problem of institutional choice is not necessarily a straightforward government versus market issue. Thus his criticisms of the tort system reflect a general scepticism concerning the ability of an institution using a case-by-case approach to arrive at the 'correct' solution. The corollary of his arguments that general rules, such as 'caveat emptor', should not be rigidly applied in all situations, is the need for an institution capable of deciding on an activity basis rather than on a case-by-case basis. However, we do not wish to pursue this line of analysis any further, since, as we shall suggest in chapter 7, the choice and design of such an institution is largely an empirical question upon which theoretical welfare economics (as opposed to positive economics and cost benefit analysis) can provide little guidance.

6.3 Industrial accidents

The main problem[13] with the economic analysis of industrial personal injuries is that, unlike road accidents, they are heterogenous. They are classified under ten broad headings in the official statistics in the UK for accidents at work, which again, leave out about 20 per cent of the work force because '... they do not fall within scope of any occupational safety and health legislation'.[14] All these groups themselves can be subdivided into various subgroups. But most of them, like accidents in factories, in docks, in warehouses and in construction, are so different from one case to the other even within a group that ' ... some kind of standard formula to assist employers to estimate their accident costs' becomes difficult to formulate. Accidents at work are costly to the employers, to the victims (usually employees), to the insurance companies and to the Exchequer. Prevention of accidents is also costly to the employers and to the Inspectorate of Factories and other safety organisations. Resources to meet these costs are not unlimited. Therefore, a cost-benefit analysis is useful here to evaluate how effective are the different preventive measures to reduce the accident costs.

But a cost-benefit analysis of accidents at work presupposes that preventive measures are effective in a non-random manner. Unlike other related cases of cost-benefit analysis, environmental pollution for example, in accident prevention the precise effectiveness of preventive measures are not beyond doubt. To put it differently, accidents at work may or may not follow any pattern; if they do not, the effectiveness of all preventive measures would be random. If there is a pattern to some kind of accidents at a certain form of work, discovery of this pattern could be advantageously used in preventive measures. Some accidents may follow a pattern, whereas others may be entirely random. The knowledge of a pattern like this could still be useful, in any particular type of accident at work in an industry.

There is a corresponding legal problem here which has been aptly noted by the Robens Committee Report, chapter 17, 'Compensation and Prevention'. The committee noted, during its investigations that it was '... impossible to ignore the interplay between the compensation arguments and the accident prevention arrangements ...' and '... that the present system of civil actions against damages for industrial accidents, whatever its other merits or demerits, has an inhibiting and distorting effect on the work of making and enforcing effective regulations to prevent accidents...'. The committee is of the opinion that the legal set-up of compensation is such that '... attention is diverted from the primary objective of accident prevention to the altogether different question of compensation for injury suffered.' What is most disturbing however, is that, '... judicial interpretations in compensation cases have from time to time created (or exposed) problems in the application and scope of particular accident prevention regulations.' Clearly, this is a case for organising law and its interpretation in the context of the broad economic principle of equality of the fulfilment of different objectives (viz. prevention and compensation) on the margin. A reorganisation of laws in this context in relating preventive and compensating measures at all levels could be, in the long run, more productive than a few million spent on either preventive mechanisms or compensatory arrangements.

Another problem of accidents in general is that accidents are a kind of joint product; they cause both personal injury and damage to equipment. In many cases they are separated, but mostly they happen concurrently. Accidents thus cause damages of varying degrees to human and real capital. In the absence of slavery, however, people who suffer damage to human capital are usually different from the party who suffers loss of real capital. This distinction is important in preventive measures, if we are interested only in the personal injury part, as in this case, because prevention of accidents would have some benefits for the real capital as well. In insurance against the liability for damages, the distinction becomes specially important.

To quote the Robens Report:

> With the spread of liability insurance – recently reinforced by the Employers' Liability (Compulsory Insurance) Act 1969 which came into effect in January 1972 – common law damages are almost never paid by the person liable at law for the injury. Nor is much hard evidence available to indicate that liability insurance premiums paid by individual employers – as distinct from the general level of such premiums – are adjusted to any very significant extent in the light of claims experience (p. 146).

The Report continues:

> In general, our impression is that direct contribution of the insurance companies to good safety and health performance lies more in the field of insurance against damage to premises, plant and equipment. Not only do various premiums appear to be more extensively used in this area ... but various types of direct preventive activities are undertaken ... It is apparent, therefore, that in some areas the insurance industry is making a valuable contribution towards higher

standards of safety and health at workplaces. Nevertheless, we suspect that considerable room remains for developing further ways and means of counteracting the disincentive effect of the basic principle of 'spreading the risk'.

Thus, so far as preventive measures for accidents are distinguishable between damages to human and non-human capital, the insurance industry seems to have been a damper to the personal accident prohibitive incentives on behalf of the employer. The problem to a typical firm may be looked at as follows. The real cost of a personal injury to an employer is the cost of temporary disorganisation of the production process. If this is likely to be more costly than the cost of some preventive measure, the entrepreneur may buy such measure himself, given the situation that insurance premiums do not vary much with claims records in the cases of personal injury. If it does, then there is a choice on the margin between self-protection and buying insurance of a certain proportion of total damages. It could be desirable for society as a whole, if insurance premiums against the chances of paying compensation for common law damages by the employers are made directly variable with respect to claims records in all cases of personal injury.

On the statutory part of the payments for personal injury the Robens Report also recommends '. . . differential rates of employers' contribution based on claims experience, taking into account experience of the operation of such schemes in other countries' (p. 199). The Report also feels the need to integrate accident prevention provisions with those for compensation. We have already noted the basic conceptual difficulties of cost-benefit analysis for such a scheme of accident prevention and compensation due to the (i) heterogeneity of accidents at work and (ii) accidents being a 'joint product' causing damages both to human and non-human capital. Let us now turn to the problems of measuring these accidents.

6.4 Statistical information

The main problem of analysing statistical data on industrial accidents (or accidents at work) lies in its heterogeneity even in a single industry. This very feature has been responsible for the limited success in compiling comparable time-series data on occupational accidents. This is illustrated by the complexity of the annual figures which provide the statistical background for '. . . public discussion of trends in safety and health at workplace . .' (see, for example, Tables 1 and 2 in the Robens Report). But there are problems with the data even after they are available, because they may not account for all the accidents sustained at work. The published data are '. . by-products of the information system designed to produce material for the accident prevention work.' They are the products of the priorities and the plan and work strategy of the inspectorates who are more interested in the '. . . range and coverage than in numerical accuracy'. Evidence of the lack of reliability in the accident data collected from the records of the safety inspectorates may be found in similar information from the Department of Health and Social Security data for the annual claims for industrial injury benefit. There is considerable discrepancy between the data from this source and those published by the inspectorates. There are some identifiable causes behind this anomaly, which, nonetheless, make the use of available statistical information all the more difficult.

The problem is more acute in cases of slight injuries than those of severe injuries. There are two serious obstacles to any rational interpretation of time series data on the first type of occupational accidents. The first is suggested by a survey carried out by the Factory Inspectorate, which suggests that, in manufacturing industry '. . . more than a quarter of accidents legally notifiable under the Factories Act are not in fact notified' (Robens Report, p. 135). Secondly, '. . . the usual criterion of notification – absence from work for more than three days – . . . is affected by changes in social attitudes to, and social provision for, sickness absence.' Thus, small changes either in under-reporting or in attitudes to sickness absence might considerably affect data on this account which may bear no relation to the safety performance of the industry.

There seems to be two types of heterogeneity of occupational accident data which one has to tackle before any sensible quantitative discussion may start on this subject. The first one is that of the type of injury. There is no confusion about the data of fatalities. On serious and minor injuries, however, the duration of sickness absence could provide a measure of the severity of damage. But we have already noticed the problems of under-reporting and of social attitude on the second type of accidents here. The Robens Committee prefer an objective medical criterion for the first (p. 135). But, to make the concept of personal injury measurable, it seems gross loss of earnings due to the damage could be used for both slight and serious injuries. In serious injuries, however, there is an element of loss of human capital which may have to be assessed in the calculation of compensation for personal damages suffered at work. This stock of value may be added to the loss of gross earnings to estimate the severity of damage. For fatal accidents, a money value of human life, already attempted both at theoretical and empirical level, may be used to measure the loss. The obvious advantage of measuring all kinds of personal injury – from the three-day sickness absence due to slight injury, to the loss of life – through the measuring rod of flows of income – lies in these disservices being homogeneous and their homogeneity could be immensely useful for analytical and therefore, ultimately, for policy purposes. The conceptual defence for using gross loss of income as a measure of injury may lie with the supposedly profit maximising firms equating wages to marginal revenue products, so that when an injury occurs, the loss may be said to be equivalent to the gross loss of earnings during the period of sickness absence, though neither the firm nor the accident victim actually suffers the entire loss, thanks to the statutory industrial injury benefit, common law payments, sick pay and insurance against such losses.

6.5 Some economic works on industrial accidents

The problems enumerated in the last section for an economic analysis of industrial accidents have not deterred economists interpreting and studying industrial safety and many empirical regularities observed in the accident records of different industries. We discuss two such attempts, one in the US and the other in the UK, in order to sample economic research on industrial accidents. The first work we look into is by Walter Oi 'On the Economics of Industrial Safety'.[15]

Oi starts with a theory where accidents are inherent in the process of production and no action by employees or workers can change the injury risk. He then relaxes this assumption and enquires into an equilibrium rate of accidents which may differ from socially optimal rates. Oi also looks into some empirical works on regularities observed in industrial accidents, such as: (i) how injury rates vary directly with economic activity; (ii) how stable the dispersion of injury rates is between different industries; (iii) how age and sex differentials affect injury rates; (iv) how labour turnover affects injury rates and (v) how firm size affects injury risks. He considers these empirical regularities as '... suggestive of some of the properties of the technological trade-offs between injuries and goods'. Next, Oi examines the social policies on industrial safety in terms of his equilibrium rate of injury risks and also under the supposition that such policies are to be judged as changing the equilibrium rate towards the socially optimal rate.

Oi's first theory of inherent injury risks starts in a two commodity world where one industry is totally riskless while the other is risky. Since accidents cannot be avoided in this kind of world there may not be any accident prevention costs, but accident costs could be reduced by diverting labour from the risky to the riskless industry. This diversion need not necessarily imply a move for the better because consumers have a certain kind of preference for both the goods and this preference pattern may be depicted by an indifference map. Accident costs would also vary according to the risk-disposition of the workers. For example, risk aversion would lead to a demand for some risk premium which would more than compensate for the expected loss of income due to a possible injury. Next, Oi considers a transformation curve between the two goods and sets it against the indifference map to find out the 'bliss' point which indicates the optimal bundle of goods to be produced and consumed, the allocation of labour in the two industries and also '. . . an optimum level of industrial safety which maximises consumer welfare'. An excise tax on the risky goods would reduce accident costs and move the optimum point away from the earlier 'bliss' point. This would cause a divergence between the marginal rate of substitution and the marginal rate of transformation between the two goods resulting in a higher marginal valuation of the risky goods than the '. . . opportunity cost (including the cost of more injuries) of producing more of . . .' the risky goods. According to Oi, accident prevention cost in this context may be visualised from this loss of consumer preference level. Oi also considers risk aversion, insurance and information about risk differentials to examine whether market equilibrium will coincide with the 'bliss' point. One of his important conclusions, even in this preliminary model, indicates that the 'assignment of liability for accident costs' has no bearing on the level of equilibrium injury rates.

Oi extends his theory by assuming that the frequency of industrial accidents could be altered, up to a limit, by the actions of the employers and workers. He considers injury as part of a joint product along with goods. There are different kinds of safety inputs like slow rate of production, safety engineers, guards etc. These safety inputs could be so arranged that the firm's safety expenditure(S) is minimised for a certain rate of injury risk. Again, the injury risk may rise if employment is increased for a given level of S, '. . . because the firm now spends less on industrial safety for each worker'. Oi then goes on to derive an accident prevention or safety curve for a given level of employment, where he relates safety expenditure inversely with the injury risk. This safety curve would vary '. . . across firms and industries, being higher for the innately more hazardous industries'. He then sets it against the accident cost which includes loss of non-human capital, 'disruptions of production schedules', higher wages that may have to be offered for a high injury record, etc., and works out the equilibrium injury rate for the firm from the marginal condition to minimise the sum of the accident and accident prevention cost. Oi next compares this equilibrium rate with the socially optimal rate under different sets of compensation rules, absence of full information, and contributory negligence. He admits that his specification of the problem is in terms of partial equilibrium and refers to some work where both the demand for and supply of labour are derived with the injury risk being an endogenous variable. Oi concludes his theoretical sections with the idea of a general equilibrium specification of this accidental injury problem where changing consumers' preference for risky goods and services may be brought to bear on the move towards a socially optimal level of work injuries.

In contrast to Oi's work the other piece of research is more specific in its application but its theoretical formulation looks ad hoc in comparison. This is the paper by G.R. Steele on 'Industrial accidents: an economic interpretation'.[16] Steel starts with an analogy between men and machines: 'If we assume a work-period of standard length (hours per year) then non-work time – tea and lunch breaks, rest periods, holidays, etc. – can be taken as time for recompensation (and hence maintenance). Overtime working is then to be regarded as the neglect of maintenance.' From this starting point Steele builds up his model which leads to four hypotheses, based on some suitable assumptions. He then goes on to test these four hypotheses on the basis of recent British industrial experience. Steele's hypotheses are: (i) 'marginal accident rate will equal the average accident rate'; (ii) 'industrial injuries will vary inversely with the degree of labour scarcity'; (iii) '... accidents and employment will vary inversely'; (iv) 'industrial injuries will vary directly with the amount of overtime working.' These hypotheses are tested on time series and cross-section data and they are found to be consistent with the data, some more than others. Yet the formulation of the theory on this basis of an anology remains rather ad hoc. For social policy issues it would be more satisfactory to start from a particular welfare paradigm such as Oi's.

In section 6.2 in our discussion of product liability, we noted that the application of economics to accident analysis is considerably easier in situations where property rights are reasonably well defined. Just as with the purchase and use of products where we adapted existing market paradigms, Oi's treatment of industrial accidents is facilitated by the presence of a market for labour services into which may be inserted the special problems of accidental injury. We may contrast this market based analysis with our own model presented in chapter 4 which should largely be seen as an exercise in optimisation for a public agency in a situation such as road safety where the high transaction costs make a market solution highly impractical.

Notes

1 Even single vehicle, driver only accidents may be included in this generalisation.

2 I. Illich, *Medical Nemesis: the expropriation of health*, Calder and Boyars, London 1975.

3 R. Nader, *Unsafe at any Speed*, Grossman, New York, 1965.

4 W. Y. Oi, 'The Economics of Product Safety', *The Bell Journal of Economics and Management Science*, vol. 4, no. 1, Spring 1973, pp. 3–28.

5 J. M. Buchanan, 'In Defence of Caveat Emptor', *University of Chicago Law Review*, vol. 38, Fall 1970, pp. 64–73.

6 R. N. McKean, 'Products Liability: Trends and Implications,' *University of Chicago Law Review*, vol. 38, Fall 1970, pp. 3–63.

7 W. Y. Oi, op. cit., p. 17.

8 V. Goldberg, 'The Economies of Product Safety and Imperfect Information', *The Bell Journal of Economics and Management Science*, vol. 5, no. 2, Autumn 1974, pp. 683–8.

9 W. Y. Oi, 'The Economics of Product Safety: a rejoinder', *The Bell Journal of Economics and Management Science*, vol. 5, no. 2, Autumn 1974.

10 R. Dorfman, 'The Economics Product Liability. A Reaction to McKean', *University of Chicago Law Review*, vol. 38, 1970–71, pp. 74–91.

11 G. Calabresi, 'Right Approach, Wrong Implications; A Critique of McKean on Products Liability, *University of Chicago Law Review*, vol. 38, 1970–71, pp. 92–102.

12 J. M. Buchanan, *Cost and Choice: an inquiry in economic theory*, Markham, Chicago 1969.

13 D. Ghosh and D. Lees, 'Cost and Compensation for Personal Injuries in Industrial Accidents: A case study', Discussion Paper no. 18 in *Discussion Papers in Industrial Economics*, Department of Industrial Economics, University of Nottingham, February 1975.

14 Lord Robens, *Safety and Health at Work*, Report of the Committee 1970–72, HMSO, July 1972, p. 161.

15 W. Y. Oi, 'On the Economics of Industrial Safety', *Working Paper 48, Industrial Relations Section*, Princeton University, June 1974.

16 G. R. Steele, 'Industrial accidents: an economic interpretation', *Applied Economics*, 1974, vol. 6, pp. 143–55.

7 The economics of compensation

7.1 Accidental injury as a social problem

One possible criticism of the economic approach as we have outlined it up till now is that the whole perspective of the social problem is distorted by concentrating on the deterrence of accidents rather than on the amelioration of the suffering of the accident victims and their dependents. A social administrator, for example, may be extremely sceptical about the empirical relevance of the first law of demand as an instrument of accident prevention. From his viewpoint, the hub of the social problem would probably be the need exhibited by the accident victims rather than the theoretical desirability of making the full costs of an activity internal to the participants in the activity.

If, however, we do change the emphasis of our concern, we are faced with new questions to which economics per se can provide very few answers. Indeed, the very term 'compensation' may itself be inappropriate where the emphasis of policy is on the need of the injured and disabled person rather than on the cause of the accident. How, for example, can we justify full financial restriction of disabled accident victims when the disability stemming from congenital effect or disease is treated as a problem of an overall welfare system which awards benefits on a far less generous basis? Is there any reason to treat the accident victim as a special case in social policy if we choose to break the connection between compensations and accident causation?

Many economists would argue that the answers to these questions can only stem from a stronger and more comprehensive value system than is implied by the behavioural and ethical postulates of economic theory. More specifically, they might argue that compensation per se is a problem of equity rather than efficiency. This is an issue which we discuss in the early sections of this chapter where we hope to show that even the individualistic Paretian approach can be applied to the problems of loss-spreading and that it may be used both to explain and to prescribe on a compensation policy. In the second half of the chapter we present two examples of the sort of detailed empirical work which we feel is a necessary adjunct to our theoretical ruminations.

7.1.2 *Loss-spreading: equity or efficiency?*

In the previous sections we have seen how a different perspective on the problem of injury and disability can lead to a quite different policy emphasis. With much of the economics literature and a large portion of this book seemingly concerned with arriving at an 'efficient' level of accidents, the reader may be excused for expecting an apparent incompleteness from a social policy based on economic reasoning. The 'gap' in the policy clearly occurs because, as we explained in chapter 4, an optimal level of accidents is unlikely to be the same as a zero level of accidents. Furthermore, while the victims and their dependents may be compensated as a by-product of the accident cost internalisation process, there is no reason why, in principle, the victims may themselves be the cheapest accident avoiders and must therefore bear the full costs of the misfortune unaided. This possibility is clearly envisaged by R. N. McKean[1] who feels that a distinction must be preserved between the efficiency objective and the equity objective.

The value of this distinction in the particular context of accident policy would seem to be open to doubt since as we have seen the efficiency objective identified by our aggregative loss function is not the pure Paretian efficiency as defined in section 4.2.2. Since interpersonal comparisons of utility are required to identify the cheapest accident avoider it might seem inconsistent to eschew them in developing a policy of accident compensation.

Calabresi's framework clearly considers that loss-spreading or 'secondary cost minimisation' is an important objective of social policy and that any ideal system of accident law needs to reconcile the possible trade-offs between loss-spreading and primary cost minimisation.[2] While we agree with Calabresi that in the design of an institutional response to accidental damage we will have to combine these two goals, we will initially consider the general economic aspects of loss-spreading without the additional complication of engineering an optimal level of accidents.

One way of evading the problem of pre-accident externalities is to assume a situation where transaction costs do not preclude the attainment of an efficient level of accidents in the Coasian sense but not to assume that information is complete or that uncertainty is absent. Alternatively, we may assume that the distribution of property rights has exogenously adapted to the presence of accident externalities and that the resulting liability rules define a Paretian region along the lines suggested by J. M. Buchanan[3] where it is ignorance and uncertainty rather than externality that is hindering the attainment of optimality. Neither assumption affects the theoretical welfare economics of insurance provision. However, as we shall see in section 7.2.1, there are important empirical differences between the costs of, say, liability insurance and personal accident insurance.

In chapter 4, whilst we did discuss the difference between the ex ante and ex post perception of accident costs, we were solely interested in the externality relationship between accident victims and/or injurers. If we now assume that the accident generating externality relationship is perceived ex ante then we may call this a pre-accident externality. The purpose of introducing this extra concept is to distinguish between externalities relating to accident causations and those relating to the *compensation* of accident victims which as we shall see may often be experienced by parties who are completely independent of the accident generation process. This type of accident externality we will define as being a post-accident externality – a concept which we will develop further in section 7.1.4.

In section 7.1.3. we aim to consider an economic approach to loss-spreading which could in principle subsume the problem of post-accident externalities but which in the cause of greater simplicity we choose to ignore (but see M. V. Pauly[4]).

7.1.3 *Loss-spreading and the economics of insurance*

Having made the above assumptions concerning pre-accident externality we can return to our individualistic model of society and apply the methodology outlined in chapter 4 in order to guide our choice of allocative mechanism. Once again we may assume that the predominant form of allocation is competitive markets and that the justification for non-market allocation must be derived from some form of market failure in the particular instance in this case of insurance. We will, however, follow a slightly different approach and, by postulating an 'ideal provision of insurance', consider the economic problems that any allocative device must face. We will also suggest that 'ideal' insurance is not the same as optimal insurance.

One assumption implicit in this section is the behavioural postulate that individuals are generally risk averse. This means that an individual will prefer to pay a certain sum x rather than face the prospect of a probability distribution of losses with a mean of x.[5] This is the general welfare argument for the provision of insurance. It would be fallacious, however, if we ignored the economic problems of the supply of insurance services which so many writers on social policy seem to neglect. In many cases it is easy to identify a potential 'need' for reducing uncertainty through the provision of insurance (particularly social insurance) without considering whether extra insurance is really justified on the criterion of economic efficiency.

The theoretical basis for the position of insurance is the reduction in risk afforded by the working of the law of large numbers. With respect to an insurance policy this predicts that the relative variance of a number of pooled risks declines as the number of independent risks in the pool increases. So far we have suggested theoretical reasons for the demand for insurance and for the voluntary supply of insurance. It will emerge, however, that the advantages of actuarially fair insurance are somewhat diluted in the real world of positive transaction costs. We will explain their importance by returning to our notion of 'ideal' insurance.

Ideal insurance has two important characteristics:[6]

1 It is based on the maximum discrimination of risk. In other words, for each insured risk the premium equals the actuarially predicted cost for the particular risk.

2 It is available at actuarially 'fair' rates whereby the premium is set at the point where the marginal evaluation of the individual of the insurance equals its marginal cost prior to the completion of the insurance contract. If the premium is based on the expected cost of the risk after the completion of the contract then it will be higher since the existence of insurance changes the objective probability of the calamitous event occurring.

Both market and non-market insurance provision in practice invariably involves imperfect risk-rating since it is simply too expensive in terms of information costs to assess each risk on an individual basis. Thus liability insurance typically uses broad insurance groups within which individuals with different accident probabilities are lumped together. In other words, in a world of positive information costs ideal insurance cannot be considered to be optimal insurance.

The second requirement of actuarially fair premiums based on an ex ante estimation of expected costs (the change in the probability of, for example, the accident occurring) will require that on efficiency grounds the insurer should charge a higher premium than P^*. This is illustrated in Figure 7.1.

For some risks the increase in the probability of a loss occurring might increase so much that a market for insurance will simply fail to emerge. Thus it is not generally possible to insure a business against a fall in profits or for an individual to insure his income against unemployment. Different

Figure 7.1
The impact of moral hazard on insurance premiums

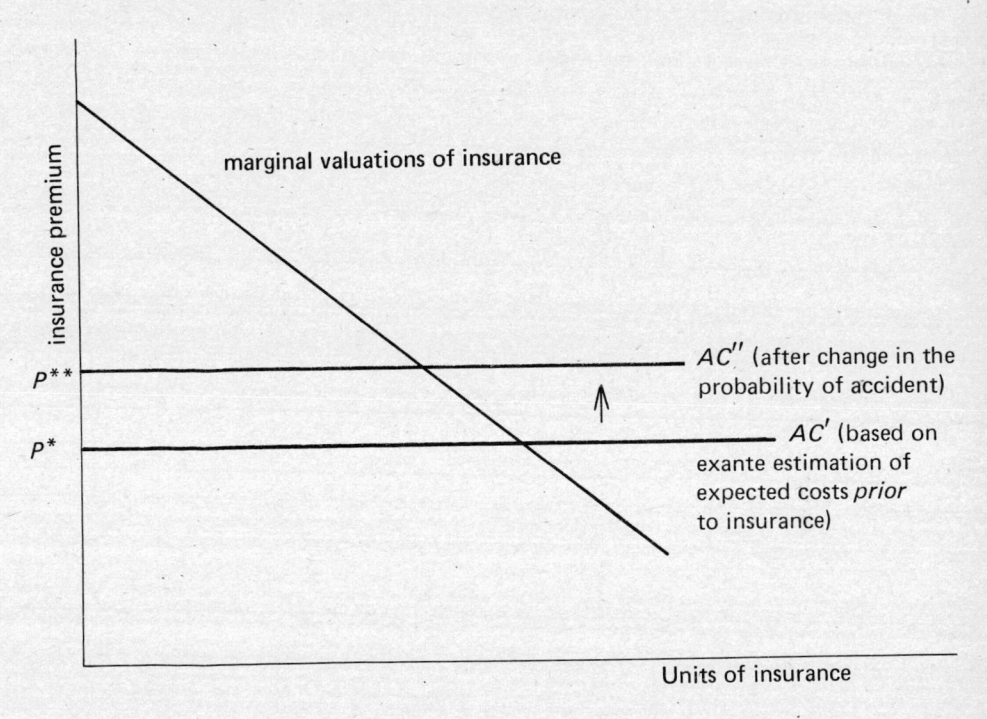

institutions have different ways of limiting the problem of moral hazard. Private insurers generally draw up a variety of contracts which may include an element of co-insurance and/or have a deductible (i.e. the insured pays a limited amount of the total loss). Under the tort system, while the courts help to enforce liability insurance contracts they do not provide any incentives for the tortfeasor to minimise moral hazard. Indeed, it is one of the standard criticisms of the tort system that the deterrence effect of the liability payment has been weakened by the development of liability insurance. The behavioural basis of moral hazard is illustrated formally by the utility function underlying our 'supply' of accidents in our model in chapter 4. It may be seen from equation (4.9) that a reduction in the loss of permanent income (f) will lead to an increase in the supply of potentially dangerous situations (X).

The problems we have isolated are not unique to any particular institution arrangement. They may lead to market failure, as suggested by Arrow, but they do not indicate on theoretical grounds an unambiguously superior system of allocation. There may be empirical, cost-benefit reasons for preferring government to private market provision but a free lunch[7] is unlikely. For example, compulsory social insurance financed through the tax system may economise on many of the transaction costs of private insurance but such a system will fail to account for individual differences in risk aversion and the consequent excess burden must be considered a deadweight social loss to be balanced against the cost savings (see 7.2.1. for fuller discussion and presentation of empirical evidence).

7.1.4 *Loss-spreading and post-accident externalities*

Economic man is usually characterised or caricatured as an individual who is preoccupied with his own material wellbeing. In many areas such an assumption has contributed to a certain amount of predictive success. Yet there is no reason inherent in the economic method which limits economic analysis to selfish behaviour. The general assumption is merely that the individual maximises a utility function. It does not preclude this function from containing arguments about other people's welfare. In other words, we cannot rule out the possibility of interdependence between individual utility functions.

The device of interdependent utility functions may be adopted for both normative and positive theories. In positive economics they have been used to explain much non-market allocation of resources while in normative economics they have extended the scope of the Paretian norms to the evaluation of a limited degree of redistribution. Indeed, given our definition of a Pareto relevant externality (see 4.1.4.) it may be seen that accident externalities are merely a special case of utility interdependence. Thus, if, following J. M. Buchanan and C. W. Stubblebine[8] an externality is defined to be present when

$$U^A = U^A (X_1, X_2, \ldots X_m, Y_1) \qquad (7.1)$$

and when

$$U^B = U^B (Y_1, Y_2, \ldots Y_m) \qquad (7.2)$$

we need not specify what activity Y_1 involves. It may be reckless driving by B which imposes external cost on A. Alternatively, it may be B's consumption of health care or education which A might wish to increase. To ensure that the externality is Pareto relevant we must clearly impose some restrictions on the utility function (see Buchanan and Stubblebine).[9] Before we consider the normative implications, let us first examine the explanatory power of interdependent utility functions in the specific context of personal injury.

As we pointed out in the first section of this chapter, the emphasis of our book on the optimal level of accidents is not found in many of the legal and sociological works on accident compensation. This literature stresses the need to help the accident victim and frequently feels that the compassion of society for these accident victims is too self evident to require discussion (but see G. Tullock).[10] Casual empirical observation certainly suggests that accidents, particularly if they are well publicised, normally generate a great increase in co-operative and charitable behaviour. L. D. Alessi[11] uses the notion of interdependent utility functions to explain the increase in post-disaster charity. Clearly social policy is rather more concerned with the 'routine' accident than with the disaster. We feel, however, that Alessi's approach may be applied to the accident victims in general with the acknowledgement that disasters tend to generate more widespread voluntary giving simply because the perception of the need of these victims is much more widespread. In other words, the publicity surrounding the major disaster reduces the search costs for the givers.

Alessi is careful to stress that the disaster does not cause a shift in utility functions. The interdependence between utility functions already exists. It is the dramatic changes in wealth which lead to an increase in the marginal utility of the charitable donor. We may illustrate the use of interdependent utility functions both formally and diagramatically.

Let us postulate an extremely simple interdependency in which:

$$U_A = f(W_A, W_B)$$
$$U_B = f(W_A, W_B)$$

and

$$\frac{\delta U_A}{\delta W_A} > 0 \quad \frac{\delta U_A}{\delta W_B} > 0$$

$$\frac{\delta U_B}{\delta W_B} > 0 \quad \frac{\delta U_B}{\delta W_A} > 0$$

and

$$W_A > W_B$$

and where U_A and U_B are the utilities of two individuals A and B and W_A and W_B represent their stocks of wealth respectively.[12]

Following H. H. Hochman and J. D. Rodgers,[13] we analyse how the size of the wealth transfers depends on the differential between the individuals' wealth. Thus if the effect of an accident on B is to increase the differential we may trace the effect on A in Figure 7.2.

Figure 7.2
Effect of accidental injury to B on A's equilibrium wealth transfer

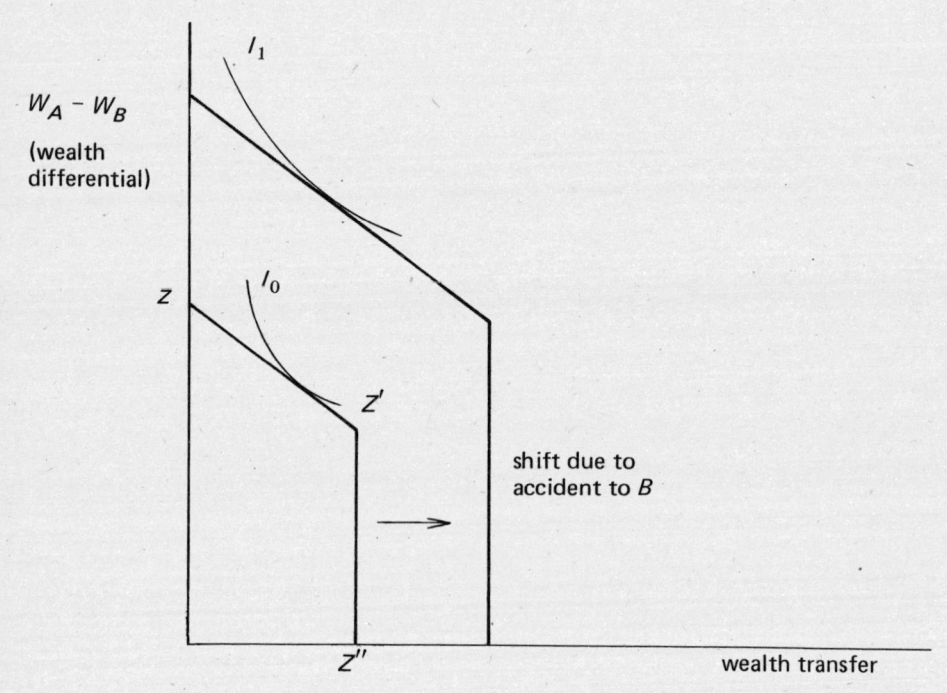

[Figure: Graph with vertical axis labeled $W_A - W_B$ (wealth differential) and horizontal axis labeled "wealth transfer". Budget line $ZZ'Z''$ with indifference curves I_1 and I_0. Arrow indicating "shift due to accident to B".]

I_1 and I_0 represent the rate at which A trades off decreases in his own wealth against increases in B's wealth. On the horizontal axis we have the wealth transfer while on the vertical axis we have the difference between A's wealth and B's wealth. The line $ZZ'Z''$ represents a budget line which shifts in response to changes in the relative wealth levels. Thus if B suffers an accident there will be a parallel shift to the right in $ZZ'Z''$. The new equilibrium level of transfer will depend upon A's transfer elasticity which in our diagram is positive but less than one (see Hochman and Rodgers[14] for discussion of other cases.)

One characteristic of charitable advertising is that the charity often stresses that its funds will not be directly transferred to the recipients but will be used to provide specific commodities deemed desirable by the donors. Thus in the case of accident victims much effort will be devoted to the provision of medical care, rehabilitation centres and home helps. Since the basis of our approach is that we are concentrating on the preferences of the donors rather than the recipients we may ignore the usual analytical result which shows that individuals prefer to receive cash rather than goods. The modification we are introducing replaces general interdependency related to wealth levels and substitutes interdependency over a specific range of goods. For example, we may write the utility functions such that:

$$U^A = U^A (x_1^A, x_2^A, \ldots, x_n^A, x_1^B) \qquad (1)$$

$$U^B = U^B (x_1^B, x_2^B, \ldots, x_n^B) \qquad (2)$$

where x_1 is a 'desirable' commodity such as a rehabilitation centre.

As we noted in chapter 4, the identification of a Pareto relevant externality does not imply any particular institutional form. Alessi was not trying to explain governmental income support per se but all forms of charitable behaviour both private and collective. Once again, in order to explain (or to justify) governmental compensation and rehabilitation policies within our individualistic model, we need to return to the public goods/isolation paradox which we drew on in 4.1.6.

Before we evaluate the policy implications of these two economic theories of compensation we might consider how compatible each theory is with observable performance of existing compensation systems. Let us first summarise the predictions of our two approaches.

Our brief excursion into the economics of insurance suggests that many risks will be uninsured by private markets. It does not suggest, however, how government can more efficiently insure these risks or, in other words, how it can reduce the transaction costs which hindered the formation of markets. It is apparent that it poorly explains the distribution of compensation by the tort system which must be a particularly incongruous system for dispensing social insurance. The desire for insurance is more evident in the statutory provisions such as workmen's compensation laws and provisions such as those in the UK which make third party liability insurance compulsory for all motorists. It may even be argued that the tort system contributes to the 'market failures' in the provision of personal accident insurance since it increases the uncertainly faced by the individual and complicates his decision calculus.

The interdependent utility function approach does not predict government intervention or redistribution in itself. It does seem to explain charitable behaviour pretty well, particularly if we include the influence of information costs on the perception of accident/disaster victims. To explain government intervention we must return to the public goods argument of chapter 4. Hochman and Rodgers[15] suggest that: 'Voluntary transfers, as within families, would likely occur in the two person case. In the N-person case, however, individuals, unless coerced, may choose to be "free-riders" and it is the incentive to behave in this way that may be viewed as the raison d'être of government.'

Even if we accept the public goods hypothesis, the pattern of cash transfers to accident victims emerging from the tort system does not accord very closely with the general income transfers predicted by the interdependent utility function approach. Since we are unenthusiastic about the ability of either of our two main theoretical approaches to explain compensation by the courts, we will digress a little in order to consider a theory which may be seen as the positive version of the normative theory of accident loss minimisation. This theory suggests that the main objective of the tort system is not redistribution or loss-spreading but the attainment of an efficient level of accidents.

The most explicit attempt to explain court decisions as a process of loss minimisation is probably Professor Posner's theory of negligence.[16] Posner argues that: 'the dominant function of the fault system is to generate rules of liability that if followed will bring about, at least approximately, the efficient – the cost justified – level of accidents and safety.'

He 'tests' this proposition by looking at the 'opinion' expressed in American appellate cases in the period 1875–1905, which in many ways represents the high tide of the negligence concept.

It is easy to see that the basic hypothesis is derived from the normative rules proposed by Calabresi, McKean and others, simply by converting the policy norm into a behavioural proposition. Just as we noted that the normative concept of efficiency lacked the precision of the pure Pareto definition, its positive counterpart is a rather too ambiguous hypothesis to test with any ease. Like the judges who made the original decisions, we must rely on utilitarian introspection to calculate social costs and benefits and it will hardly be surprising if our assessment of an efficient decision coincides with that of the judges. In other words, the theory would seem to be rather difficult to refute given our lack of objective evidence and the malleability of the concept of efficiency. To its credit the theory does explain why the courts award full financial restitution, the principle of contributory negligence, the 'standard of care' formula and other features of the tort system which generate so much criticism from those whose objectives are concerned more with the amelioration of the suffering of the victims than with the attainment of an optimal level of accidents.

Posner's theory may be related to the more general hypothesis that the courts try to evolve a set of property rights which is based on efficiency notions in contrast to statute law which frequently exhibits evidence of special pleading by various interest groups. It is beyond the scope of this book to fully explore such wide issues. However, it does seem that our earlier economic theories of compensation do explain 'statutory' attempts to spread accident losses much better than compensation through the courts. This may reflect the often expressed proposition of political economists that the incentives for government to seek efficiency objectives are low and that, as we shall see in the next section, we cannot expect 'market failure' to be automatically replaced by government success.

7.1.5 *The economics of loss-spreading and institutional reform*

In sections 7.1.3 and 7.1.4 we presented approaches that have both normative and positive versions. Since we have already discussed the explanatory power of the theories, we aim in this section to consider the policy implications of the normative forms. In more specific terms, we aim to consider whether we can recommend any institutional changes on the basis of our earlier analysis.

Arrow[17] represented one school of economic thought when, having claimed to have identified a substantial area of 'market failure' in the availability of private insurance, he made the provocative assertion that: 'The welfare case for insurance policies of all sorts is overwhelming. It follows that the government should undertake insurance in those cases where the market, for whatever reason, has failed to emerge.'

Other writers (see e.g. Buchanan,[18] Demsetz[19]) have criticised arguments for institutional reform based on the identification of 'market failure'. While we do not, of course, assume that institutional reform must only be based on notions of efficiency, the debate among economists is generally limited to the ability of a particular institutional structure to achieve a state of Pareto optimality. One immediate source of controversy lies in developing a policy relevant definition of optimality. As we have seen in chapter 4, inefficiency in the Pareto sense depends on the presence of transaction costs. We need a definition of optimality therefore that has some meaning in a real world of positive transaction costs. For example, a situation which is deemed sub-optimal in an ideal world of zero transaction costs may in fact be the best possible arrangement attainable in the self-evident presence of high transaction costs. More specifically, we cannot be sure that the market has failed if the costs of setting up market exchanges outweigh the theoretically attainable gains from trade.

Furthermore, we cannot assume on a priori grounds that we may automatically replace market failure by political or government success.

Non-market allocative devices such as collective or bureaucratic decision-making may fail for both technical and behavioural reasons. The technical obstacles to efficient governmental decision-making occur because, in the absence of markets, governments simply do not possess the necessary information on individual preferences. The behavioural obstacle to governmental success stems from the dilution of the incentives to pursue an efficiency objective in a non-market setting. In other words, the structure of property rights within government encourages officials and political representatives to pursue narrow sectional or career interests rather than maximise overall social welfare (see McKean[20]).

The technical problem of making a choice between market and non-market allocation devices is well put by Arrow[21] in a more cautious mood:

> In a price system, transaction costs drive a wedge between buyers and seller's prices and thereby give rise to welfare losses as in the usual analysis. Removal of these welfare losses by changing to another system (e.g. governmental allocation on benefit-cost criteria) must be weighed against any possible increases in transactions costs (e.g., the need for elaborate and perhaps impossible studies to determine demand functions without the benefit of observing a market.

All these caveats concerning the policy implications that may be drawn from theoretical welfare economics might seem to indicate total sterility. We have expressed pessimism concerning both the technical and normative validity of our theoretical approach as well as scepticism as to its appeal to collective decision-makers. Pauly's[22] response to the latter criticism is to suggest that: 'providing political leaders with some analysis of characteristics of optimal schemes may well be useful to them or, at least, such information may be useful to citizens who wish to evaluate political behaviour. Perhaps that is all we can expect from theory.'

It should be apparent that our discussion of institutional reform has either explicitly or implicitly been concerned with a market versus government debate. While this has relevance for the problem of loss-spreading, it is clear from the literature that the most frequent debate in accident policy is government versus tort rather than government versus market. Although we decided to temporarily ignore the problem of primary cost avoidance, most policy discussions assume that an appropriate institutional device should control accidents and also spread accident losses. In other words, we cannot divorce pre-accident externalities from the externality and insurance problems generated by the accident victim. Or in Calabresi's terminology, the minimisation of primary, secondary and tertiary costs presents a global objective with conflicting sub-goals. Although the possibility of conflicting sub-goals does not present any formal problem in global maximisation, in practical terms the problem is immense since we require a community utility function which provides us with weight for the different objectives.

7.2 The costs of compensation systems: some empirical evidence

In the second part of this chapter, we aim to show how economics may be used at a more mundane but perhaps more useful empirical level in the study of existing compensation systems. Our empirical work has not attempted the grand cost-benefit analysis implicit in Arrow's methodology of institutional choice. It follows a much more piecemeal approach in an attempt to elucidate some of the current controversies in the compensation of the accident victim.

While many aspects of the performance of compensation systems such as the dispensation of justice are clearly unquantifiable it is possible to trace in an approximate manner both the sources and the recipients of injury compensation. Such is the complexity of the various systems of compensation that it is a major task of research merely to trace and collate the flow of funds. Our own work (see Lees and Doherty[23]) has concentrated on UK data. Given the international differences in social benefit provision and compensation legislation we cannot claim that our figures indicate the relative success or failure of compensation systems in other countries. We do suggest, however, that our studies illustrate how it is possible to 'give' some sort of empirical meaning to the theoretical concepts we have introduced in this book.

In Table 7.1 for example, we compare the cost-effectiveness in terms of administration of compensation funds of the different compensation systems. It is obvious that in terms of this objective alone the UK tort system is a most ineffective performer compared with, say, the social security system. Studies in the USA indicate a similar inability of the American tort system to direct its compensation funds toward the accident victim (see A. F. Conard et al.[24]) In spite of the well documented extravagance of the legal process, it is interesting to note that it is the insurance industry which incurs the bulk of the administrative costs although, as may be seen, these costs themselves vary considerably between different types of insurance.

Table 7.1
Ratio of administrative costs to compensation

	Per cent
Tort	74
Social Security*	7
Industrial injury and disablement*	15
Life assurance	15
Personal accident insurance	55
Sick pay	5

*Includes estimate of costs of collection met by employer.

Source: D. Lees and N. Doherty, 'Compensation for Personal Injury', *Lloyds Bank Review,* April 1973, p.23.

We have called our study a 'cost-effective analysis'. This terminology is not entirely appropriate since strictly speaking it refers to a technique which measures the costs of alternative ways of achieving the same objective. In our case we cannot draw any easy conclusions from our figures since each system is producing a different 'product'. In particular, the tort system has many objectives of which compensation is but one. Since we are concerned with all these objectives, it would be naive to suggest that a switch to social insurance is indicated on the basis of Table 7.1. We have obtained some empirical estimates of what Calabresi terms 'tertiary costs' and, as he predicts, we have found that these costs increase the greater the sub-categorisation of accident causation. We have also found that, as we suspected in 6.1.4, the pooling risks and compulsory insurance — both features of social security systems — will lead to drastic reductions in transactions costs.

There is a large literature that suggests that the tort system fails equally dismally to meet its other objectives (see e.g. J. C. O'Connell[25], P. S. Atiyah[26]). We do not wish to summarise this literature or venture verdicts of our own. We merely hope to illustrate that the area of controversy is best limited to opinions and values and that questions of fact may be resolved through careful research.

7.2.2 *The quantum of damages: a case study*

One common feature of national compensation systems (with the notable exception of New Zealand[27]) is the complexity and duplication arising from the existence of overlapping systems of compensation. Thus an injured worker in the USA or UK frequently has recourse to a number of sources of financial help and compensation. The objectives of each particular system are generally well-known from official statistics and court records. However, the effect on the financial situation of the accident victim is harder to trace since public bodies have not collected the necessary data on a routine basis.[28]

In our case study[29] we have investigated the effectiveness of these systems by starting with a sample of accident victims and comparing the circumstances of the individual with the response offered by both common law and statutory compensation systems. Our data on both the losses and the compensation received were obtained from the personnel files of an accident prone industry.[30]

The data have been compiled from the files of 100 accident cases, mainly during the period 1969–72. Our sample contained only non-fatal cases of varying severity, the total sickness period ranging from less than a week to over a year. The files give a full description of the accident, the history of the case from the day of the accident to the time of settlement, and also listed calculations carried out to arrive at the damage payment figures. From those lists, we noted the following: (a) amount of settlement, (b) gross loss of earnings, (c) net loss of earnings, (d) final loss, (e) sick pay, (f) industrial injury benefits plus earnings related supplements and (g) other payments. For each accident case we also have, as already mentioned, the duration of 'total incapacitation' and of 'wait' between the day of the accident and the day of the settlement.

The amount of settlement is the final cash payment to the victim (representing the total common law payments to the victims) and it does not include any statutory payment such as (e), (f) and (g). Wherever there is a court case (such cases are less than 10 per cent in our sample), the cost is not excluded from this amount. Gross loss of earnings is calculated on the basis of gross rate of pay times the period the victim had to be absent from work. Net loss of earnings is calculated similarly, but minus the tax and the other usual payments such as national insurance.

The next figure of final loss is net loss of income less all the statutory payments that the victim receives during this period of involuntary absence from work. It should be mentioned here that, when this number is negative and there are some cases of that, a figure of zero or no loss is recorded. This does not mean that the first figure of amount of settlement is also zero in such cases – it always has some positive value. Out of 100 cases compiled by us (hopefully a representative sample of all the accidents in this industry during 1969 to 1972) thirteen had no final loss due to the accident but they all received some damage payment under common law. There could be two reasons behind this. The payment may be made for the pain and suffering due to the accident as this seems to vary roughly with the severity of the accident, measured by the duration of the forced absence from work. Payment may also be due to an impairment of human capital i.e. of future earning ability. The highest compensation payment due to an accident where the net loss of earnings and the receipts from the statutory payments add up to zero was £2,800 and there are two other similar cases when compensation of nearly £2,000 was paid to each of the victims. The payments mainly for the impairment of human capital due to the accident may be clearly indicated in two cases when a compensation of £2,800 was paid to the victim suffering a net loss of £20 in one, and in the other the similar payment was £6,000 for an opportunity cost valued at £41.

Our sample of accidental personal injury for the industry has a wide range for the compensation amounts, from £23 to £8,200. The circumstances of this wide range of compensation vary considerably. In some cases the accidents were so severe that they affected the future earnings capacity of the victims, whereas in other cases the damages caused temporary bodily and psychological distress to the victims, without causing any impairment of their human capital. It is difficult to differentiate between these two types of accident compensations. For our purposes, we have divided the sample into two groups: (a) accidents where compensation payments are less than £600 and (b) those where compensations are more than £600.

Figure 7.3 shows the distribution of accident compensations for our sample. The modal group of accident compensation has been between £101–200 and the distribution of the compensation amounts is positively skewed. Figure 7.4 depicts the distribution of the same group of accident victims in terms of their net loss of earnings due to the accidents. A glance at the two figures indicates that the level of common law compensations for accidental personal injury for this industry more or less offsets the net loss of earnings due to the forced absence from work caused by the accident. It may be noted that all cases of compensation in this group are cases of positive monetary gains due to the accidents when we add the common law payments to the statutory payments. They may be interpreted as payment for pain and suffering due to the accident, though there is not sufficient evidence here to suggest any pattern in this kind of payment. When we look at the twenty-six observations we have of the larger group of compensations (£600 plus), there is no perceptible

"Figure 7.3, Amount of settlement (max. £600)".

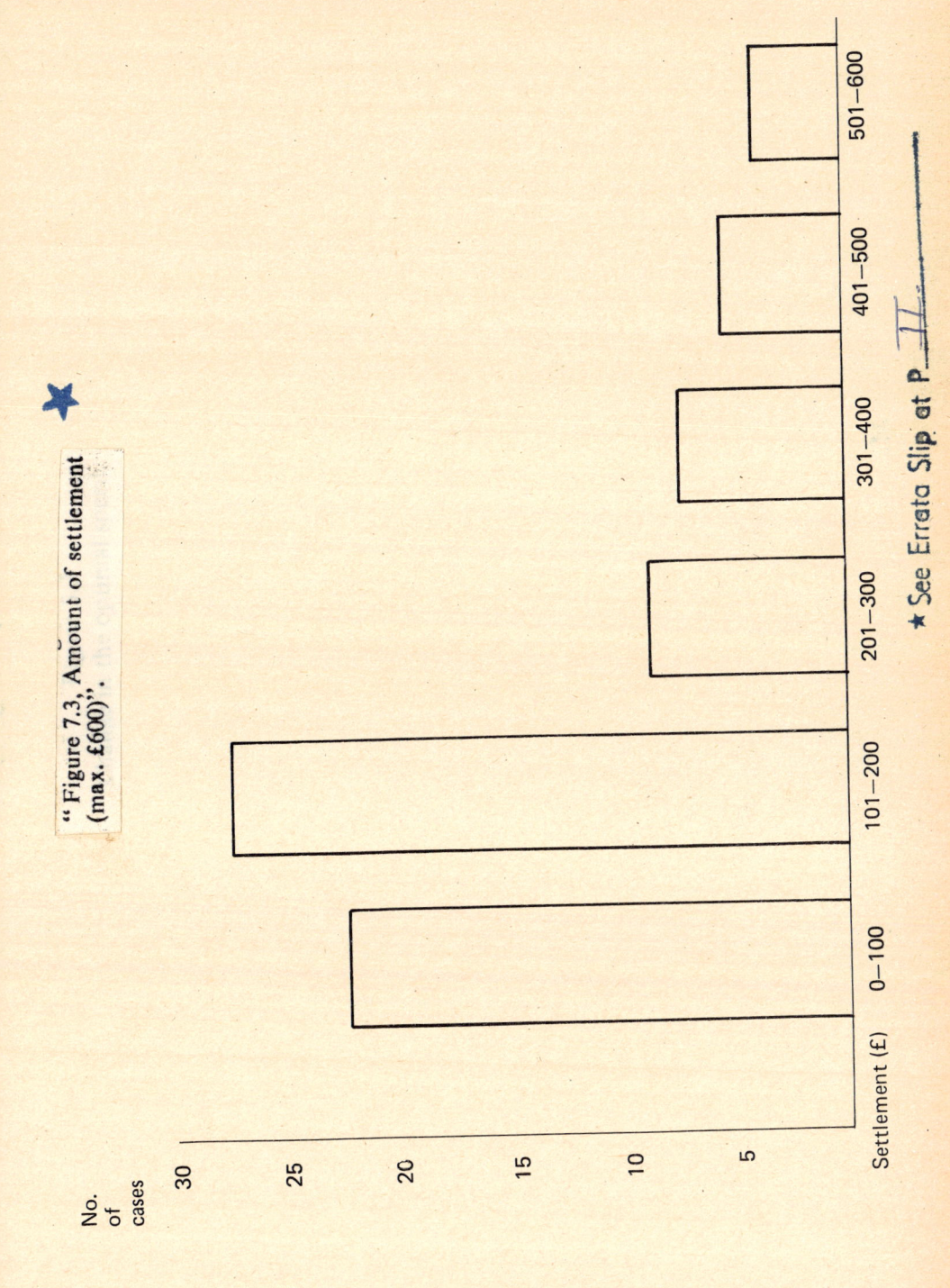

★ See Errata Slip at P. II

117

Figure 7.4
Loss of earnings (max £600)

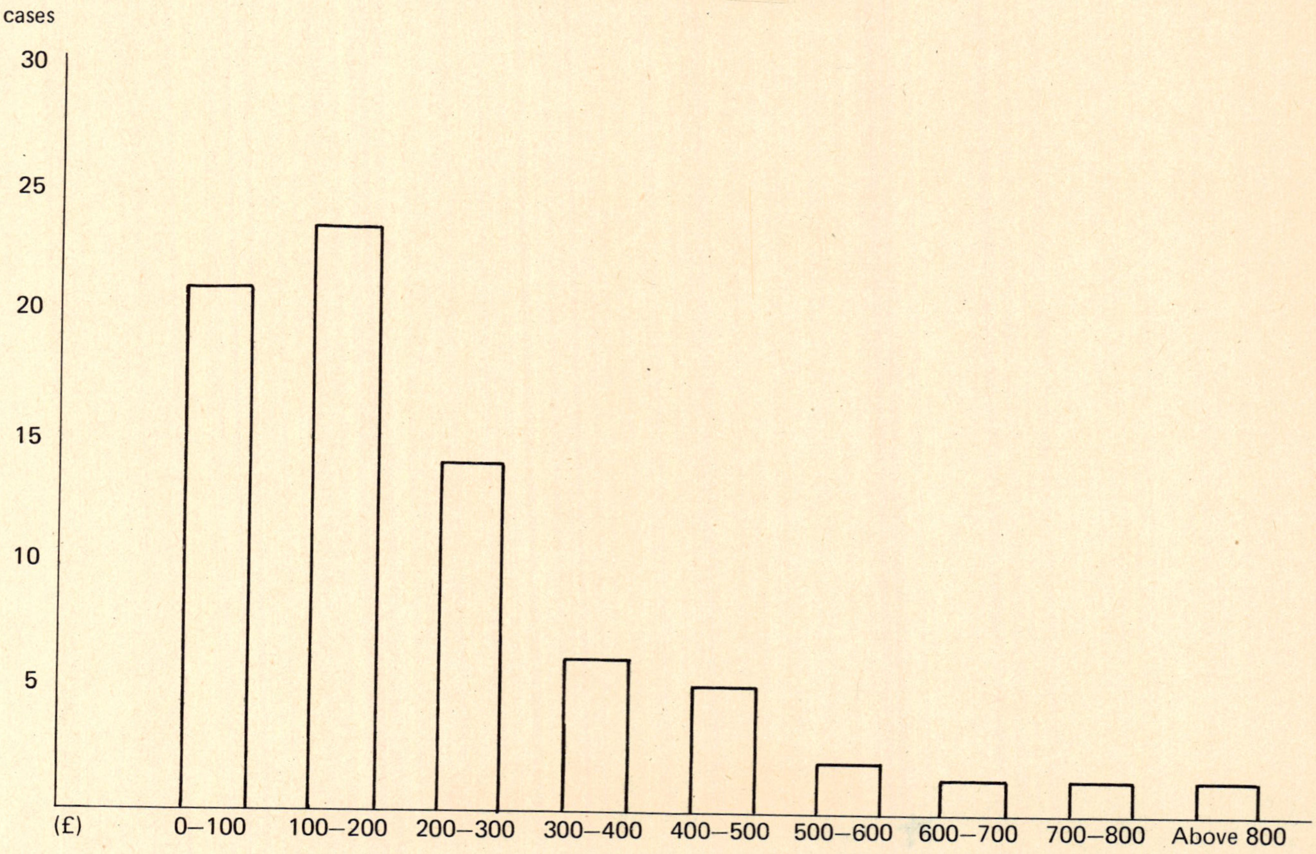

Figure 7.5
Duration of illness (**max** £600)

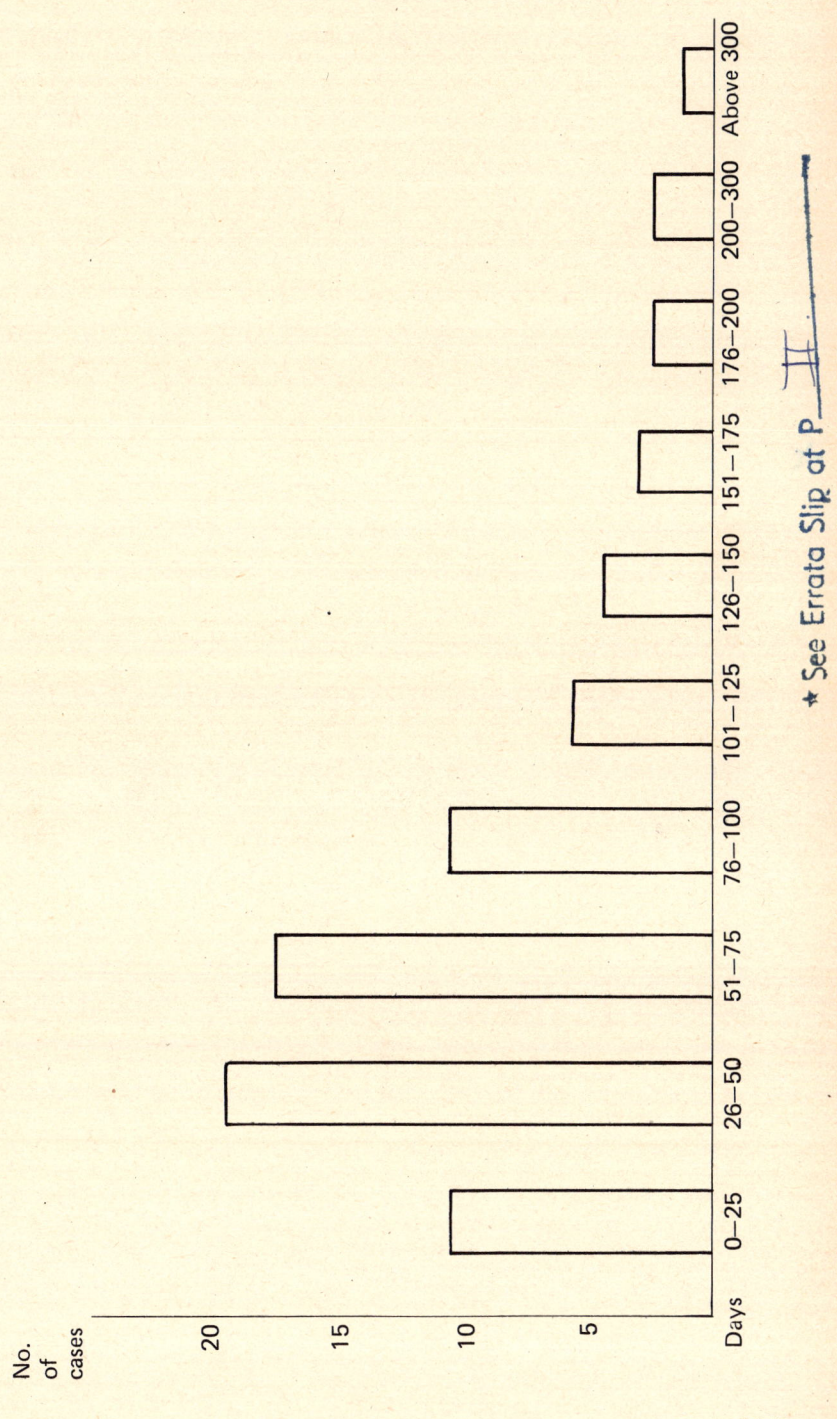

★ See Errata Slip at P.

119

Figure 7.6
Wait (days) (max £600)

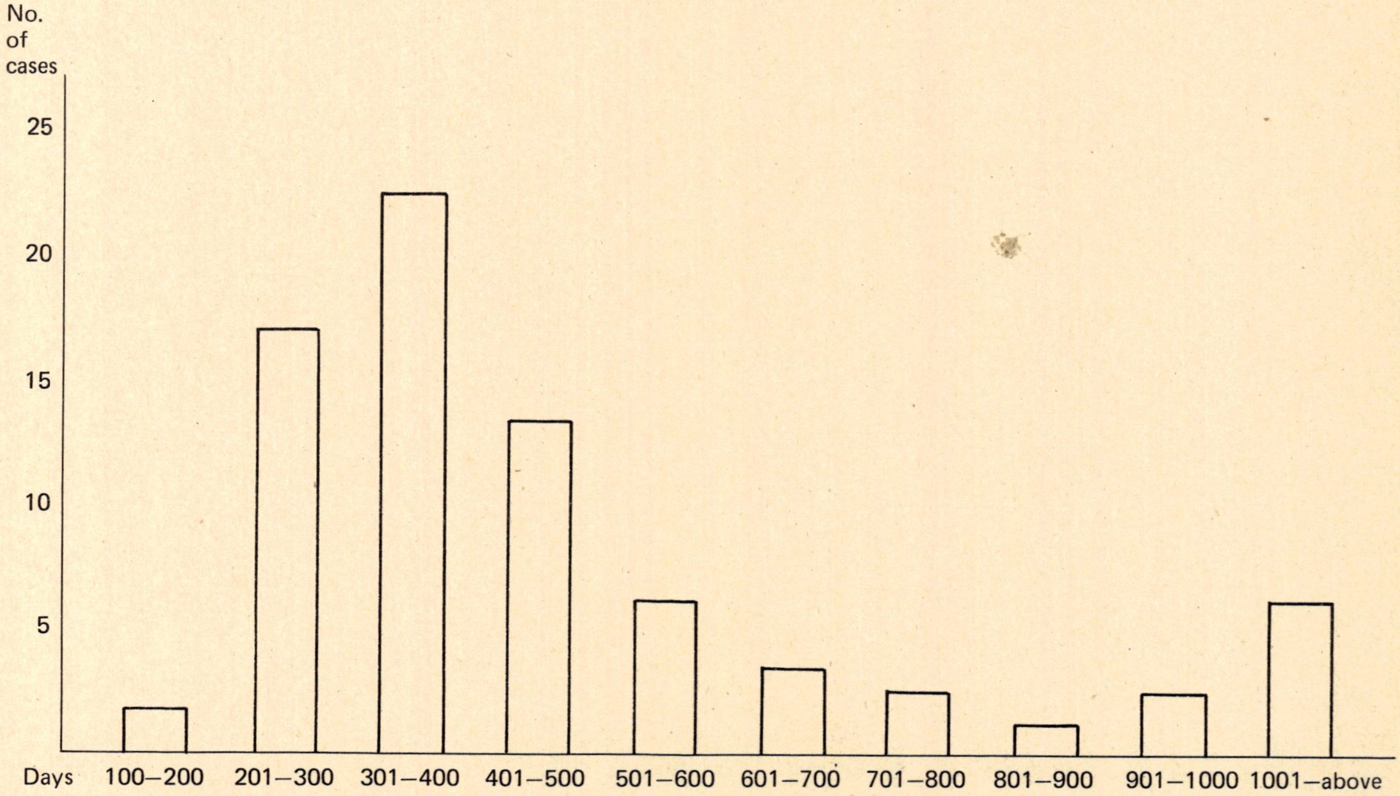

★ See Errata Slip at P. II

120

resemblance to the order noticed in Figures 7.3 and 7.4. In Figure 7.5, we present the distribution for the duration of illness due to accidents for the lower compensation group. Here the most frequent duration of illness comes out to be the period between just less than a month to less than two months, and the distribution follows a smooth pattern of positive skewness. A measure of the safety-performance of an accident-prone industry, like the one under scrutiny, could be the horizontal shift to the left of this whole distribution from period to period. This would indicate the savings made in man-days lost due to personal accidents.

Next we present a distribution of wait (in days) for receiving the common law compensation payments in Figure 7.6. Here, as in the earlier figures, we have a smooth, positively skewed distribution, the modal waiting period being between 301 to 400 days. There has been prolonged discussion on this element of compensation payment for road accident victims. Several commentators tend to consider it as part of the damage or suffering from the accident, and legislative and other measures are sometimes evaluated in terms of possible speed of payment of the damages.[31] Some delay is inescapable in any kind of payments for accidental damages due to the administrative procedures to decide on the magnitude and circumstances of an accident, even when there is hardly any reason for dispute. But when disputes do occur, the delay may be due to haggling over the extent of the damage and also over the share of the responsibility for the accident. The accident files of this industry were in many cases thick with the documents and letters from the victims' solicitors and from the employer, bargaining over the proper price of an amenity loss and also over the contributory negligence of the victims. The typical accident in this industry causes a forced absence from work for nearly one to two months, causing a typical net 'loss' of income of £100–£200 for which the victim typically receives a common law compensation payment of exactly the same amount, but for which he has to wait for 300–400 days!

Let us now look into the degree of association among various magnitudes affecting compensation, both in statutory and common law. This we can do with the help of a correlation matrix. We maintain our classification of two groups of compensation and note the zero order correlation coefficients for both of them.

From Tables 7.2 and 7.3 it is apparent that the common law payment for compensation in this industry is closely related to gross and net loss of incomes due to the accidents and also to the final loss. For the larger compensation group, however, the association between amount settled and final loss is rather low. This may suggest that compensation in this

Table 7.2

Correlation coefficients for the common law compensation group, £0–£600

	1 Wait	2 Amount settled	3 Gross loss of income	4 Net loss of income	5 Final loss	6 Sick pay	7 IIB plus ERS	8 Others	9 Duration of illness
1	1·0								
2	0·05	1·0							
3	0·25	0·72	1·0						
4	0·26	0·70	0·97	1·0					
5	0·10	0·60	0·80	0·84	1·0				
6	0·11	0·20	0·36	0·17	−0·1	1·0			
7	0·03	0·45	0·54	0·52	0·36	0·17	1·0		
8	0·41	0·34	0·50	0·52	0·33	0·07	0·07	1·0	
9	0·24	0·55	0·81	0·78	0·48	0·36	0·56	0·27	1·0

Table 7.3

Correlation coefficients for the common law compensation group, £601–£8,200

	1 Wait	2 Amount settled	3 Gross loss of income	4 Net loss of income	5 Final loss	6 Sick pay	7 IIB plus ERS	8 Others	9 Duration of illness
1	1·0								
2		1·0							
3	0·60	0·69	1·0						
4	0·57	0·66	0·98	1·0					
5	0·41	0·24	0·67	0·73	1·0				
6	0·06	−0·22	−0·60	−0·60	0·02	1·0			
7	0·12	0·30	0·35	0·35	0·11	−0·22	1·0		
8	0·29	0·66	0·63	0·63	0·07	−0·20	0·41	1·0	
9	0·68	0·15	0·66	0·66	0·53	0·16	0·18	0·38	1·0

group has been less for the past monetary loss (final loss in the tables opposite) due to the accidents, and may be more for the loss of future flows of income. The high correlation between gross and net loss of income in either group is not surprising. The three statutory payments for accidental damages, i.e. items 6, 7 and 8, do not vary closely with any other magnitude in the tables. Industrial injury benefit and earnings related supplement (item 7) are related more closely to the gross and net income loss items and also to the settlement amount in the first group than it is in the second. Again, the relations between duration of illness and the gross/net loss of earnings are closer in Table 7.2 than they are in Table 7.3. A striking difference between the two tables lies in the correlation between wait and duration of illness. If severity of damage, somehow defined, could be associated with the duration of illness, the figures might indicate that when suffering has been prolonged to cause absence from work the victims prefer to wait longer for a favourable settlement, and/or it takes a long time, through judicial procedure or otherwise, to decide how much is due for compensation for a long period of incapacitation.

Let us now look at two regression equations for the two groups, to examine how the variations in common law compensations among different cases are related to some variables in the above tables.

The estimated ordinary least square equations for the two groups are as follows:

Group I

$$X_2 = 98.76 - 0.07X_1 + 0.56X_3 - 0.24X_9$$
$$(3.79) \quad (1.66) \quad (5.96) \quad (0.63)$$
$$R^2 = .55; \quad \bar{R}^2 = .53; \quad D.W. = 1.93$$

Group II

$$X_2 = 4.04X_3 - 1.52X_5 - 4.47X_9$$
$$(8.07) \quad (2.02) \quad (3.01)$$
$$R_2 = .69; \quad \bar{R}^2 = .65; \quad D.W. = 2.14$$

(Numbers within brackets are the appropriate t-values)

The two regression equations are expressed with the help of the subscripts used above. The equation for the first group uses gross income loss (X_3), wait (X_1), duration of illness (X_9) and an intercept term as the explanatory variables whereas the second one has gross income loss, final loss (X_5) and duration of illness as the independent variables but is without an intercept term. The choice of these independent variables indicates particular points of interest, although we have eliminated other formulations through experimentation. For example, it was found that the addition of an intercept term for the second equation made only a slight contribution.

Among the significant variables, final loss and duration of illness have negative signs in the Group II equation. It may be that at this level of compensation the length of prolonged illness or the amount of final loss gradually loses its impact on the settlement figures. The important thing, however, is the predominance of gross loss of income in the explanation of settlement amount. When X_3 is used on its own with the intercept term only, R^2 comes down to ·52 in the case of Group I and to ·48 for Group II. This is an important result: it tells us *that gross loss of income is the crucial factor in the calculation of common law compensation for accidental personal damages*. Whether it is a payment for pain and suffering or a payment for the impairment of human capital affecting the future flows of income for the victim, common law compensation seems to have a single measuring rod of loss, at least in this industry.

Finally, the lack of first order autocorrelation as suggested by the Durbin—Watson statistic in either equation indicates efficient estimation for the coefficients of X_3. This may be interpreted, therefore, as a case where (i) for minor injuries when payments for pain and suffering seem to dominate the common law damages, more than 50p has been paid for a gross income loss of £1, and (ii) for serious injuries when payments for the impairment of human capital may be considered to mainly determine the settlement amounts, the payment has been more than £4 for a £1 gross income loss during the period of forced absence due to the accident.

7.3 Conclusion

In this chapter we have ranged from consideration of the theoretical basis of loss-spreading to an extremely detailed study of the treatment of the accident victim. We do not claim to have resolved any of the pressing policy issues or suggested a specific institutional response. In particular, we have not suggested how to reconcile the objective of loss-spreading with the objective of accident deterrence. Since different individuals will put different weights on each goal, we have contented ourselves with pointing out what the trade-offs are. We have also shown that these trade-offs may be given an empirical dimension to the extent that some of the entities may be represented by real financial flows.

Notes

1 R.N. McKean, 'Products Liability: Trends and Implications'. *University of Chicago Law Review,* vol. 38, Fall 1970, pp. 3–63.
2 G. Calabresi, *'Costs of Accidents',* Yale University Press, New Haven 1970.
3 J.M. Buchanan, 'The relevance of Pareto optimality', *Journal of Conflict Resolution,* vol. 6, 1962, pp. 341–54.
4 M.V. Pauly, *Medical Care at Public Expense,*Praeger, New York 1971.
5 D. Bernoulli, (English translation by L. Sommer) 'Exposition of a New Theory on the Measurement of Risk', *Econometrica,* 12, 1954.
6 K.J. Arrow, 'Uncertainty and the welfare economics of medical care', *American Economic Review,* vol. 53, 1963, pp. 941–73.
7 A 'Free Lunch' is a term applied by some economists to denote an attempt to 'get something for nothing'. See especially H. H. Demsetz's 'Information and Efficiency: Another viewpoint' *(Journal of Law and Economics,* vol. 12, pp. 1–22) for an illustration of the 'fallacy of the free lunch'.
8 J.M. Buchanan and C.W. Stubblebine, Externality', *Economica,* no. 29, 1962.
9 Ibid.
10 G. Tullock, 'The Charity of the Uncharitable', *Western Economic Journal,* vol. 8, 1970.
11 L.D. Alessi, 'The utility of disasters' *Kyklos,* vol. 21, 1968.
12 Clearly in the injury compensation area we must treat an individual's stock of human capital as the major ingredient of personal wealth. In other words, the disability following injury leads to a loss of future earnings.
13 H.H. Hochman and J.D. Rodgers, 'Pareto Optimal Re-distribution', *American Economic Review,* vol. 59, 1969.
14 Ibid.
15 Ibid.
16 R.A. Posner, 'A Theory of Negligence', *The Journal of Legal Studies,* vol. 1 (1), January 1972.
17 K.J. Arrow, op. cit. But see also D.S. Lees and R.G. Rice, 'Uncertainty and the welfare economics of medical care: comment', *American Economic Review,* vol. LV, no. 1, March, 1965, pp. 140–53.
18 J.M. Buchanan, 'Positive economics, welfare economics and political economy'. *Journal of Law and Economics,* vol. 2, pp. 124–38, 1959.
19 H.H. Demsetz, op. cit.

20 R.N. McKean, 'Property Rights within Government, and Devices to Increase Governmental Efficiency', *Southern Economic Journal*, vol. 39, 1972.

21 K.J. Arrow in 'Frontiers of quantitative economics', papers invited for presentation at the Econometric Society winter meetings, Amsterdam, North Holland, 1971.

22 M.V. Pauly, op. cit.

23 D.S. Lees and N. Doherty, 'Compensation for Personal Injury', *Lloyds Bank Review*, April 1973.

24 A.F. Conard et al. *Automobile Accident Costs and Payments: Studies in the Economics of Injury Reparation'*, Ann Arbor, 1964.

25 J.C. O'Connell, *'The Injury Industry'*, op. cit.

26 P.S. Atiyah, *Accidents, Compensation and the Law,* Weidenfeld and Nicolson, London 1970.

27 Woodhouse Report, *Royal Commission to Inquire into and Report upon Workers' Compensation,* Owen, Wellington 1967.

28 This situation is being remedied in the UK, at least, by the establishment of a Royal Inquiry into Civil Liability under the chairmanship of Lord Pearson.

29 D. Ghosh and D. Lees, 'Cost and Compensation for Personal Injuries in Industrial Accidents: A case study', Discussion Paper no. 18 in *Discussion Papers in Industrial Economics* Department of Industrial Economics, University of Nottingham, February 1975.

30 The name and type of industry has had to be withheld since the data could only be used on those conditions.

31 J.C. O'Connell, op. cit.

8 Conclusions

It is a familiar criticism of the economist's approach to policy issues that he tends to assume away the special difficulties of a problem in order to handle it with well-tried theoretical models. We hope that in this book we have avoided this temptation. In common with the best of the latest literature, we have tried to get away from economic platitudes and actually confront the accident-causing technology. To this end we proposed a method of aggregative accident analysis which measures changes in long-term trends and, in particular, measures the impact of changes in resource allocation and technological developments. We have also used our aggregative approach to measure the short-term impact of various factors such as speed and the volume of traffic. From this model we were able to predict how accident levels will move with changes in average speed and traffic volumes. The stability of our model may be retested with more recent data. We would also suggest that it would be interesting to consider explicitly the impact of the variance of traffic speeds as there is some casual empirical evidence to suggest that this has an important influence on accident levels. We have also developed a model of optimal motorway speed which is sufficiently general to handle any relationships between speed and accidents and also between speed and rate of fuel consumption. We used this model to derive some values of time and human life. In 1973 the value of time was close to the average wage and the value of life nearly £100,000. We have also enquired into the change of the optimal speed if there is a rise in the petrol price.

We may mention here that our model could be extended to consider valuation of changes in the probability of death or injury rather than a single value for life or a limb, a concept that is rightly criticised in the literature. However, until an operational valuation of changes in the probability of dying or of sustaining injury is produced, such an extension can only be of theoretical interest. For policy use, it is clear that further development of the model is hindered by the lack of empirical work carried out on the valuation problems.

Our discussions on industrial accidents mainly enumerated the problems involved in an economic investigation into this area. We proposed some method of analysing industrial accidents on the lines of a few early works already undertaken in the US. They mainly involve the discovery of some empirical regularities in the frequency or rate of industrial accidents.

Economic tenets can be applied to these phenomena to interpret behaviour or accident records as 'equilibrium' magnitudes. These equilibrium values may also be compared to another set of ideal accident rates which may be defined as socially optimal rates. Economic policy in terms of legislative and institutional rearrangements may be then evaluated in so far as the equilibrium accident rates approach the social optimal rates.

Some people may question the relevance of this excursion into welfare economics for policy issues. But without it, no conclusions can be drawn on the appropriate control of accident levels or for compensating accident victims. We do not expect to derive implications for radical institutional change from our theoretical approach but we do feel that it has enabled us to generate information with clear policy relevance. This is how we see the role of economic analysis in the formulation of social policy.

On compensation we followed a two-stage approach. Like prevention, compensation of injury involves some cost. If more resources are invested in prevention, fewer accidents are likely to occur. Our model proposes that the provision of extra compensation for accidents may induce people to indulge in more risky activities and thus reap more benefit from such endeavours. In this way one can look at resources spent on accident prevention and accident compensation as measures to reduce social disutility or, equivalently, as measures to increase social benefit. This view of compensation would indicate what its optimal level is along with the optimal levels of accident rates and of costs on prevention.

Once we know the optimal level of compensation the next set of problems on compensation is to allocate that amount efficiently among different modes and processes of compensation e.g. lump-sum or periodical payment for damages, costs for hospitalisation and after-care, etc. The most desirable solution for the optimal prevention and compensation costs lies in the simultaneous solution of all the preventive and compensatory measures along with the ways to finance them. We have not attempted in this book to solve this immense problem which could be a line of further research on accidental personal injury.

Bibliography

Ackroyd, L.W. and Bettison, M. 'Vehicle Speeds on the M1 in Nottinghamshire', *Traffic Engineering and Control*, January 1974.
Alessi, L.D., 'The Utility of Disasters', *Kyklos*, vol. 21, 1968.
Annual Reports of HM Chief Inspector of Factories, 1969–74.
Arrow, K.J., 'Uncertainty and the Welfare Economics of Medical Care', *American Economic Review*, vol. 53, 1963.
Arrow, K.J., 'Frontiers of Quantitative Economics', papers invited for presentation at the Econometric Society Winter Meetings, Amsterdam, North Holland, 1971.
Atiyah, P.S., *Accidents, Compensation and the Law*, Weidenfeld and Nicolson, London, 1970.
Becker, G.S., 'Crime and Punishment: An Economic Approach, *Journal of Political Economy*, vol 76, no. 2, 1968
Becker, G.S., 'A Theory of the Allocation of Time', *Economic Journal*, September 1965.
Bernoulli, D., (English translation by L. Sommer) 'Exposition of a New Theory on the Measurement of Risk,' *Econometrica*, 12, 1954.
British Labour Statistics, HMSO, 1972.
Brown, J.P., 'Towards an Economic Theory of Liability', *Journal of Legal Studies*, vol. 2, 1973.
Buchanan, J.M., *'Cost and Choice: An Inquiry in Economic Theory'*, Markham, Chicago, 1969.
Buchanan, J.M. and Stubblebine, W.C., 'Externality', *Economica*, vol 29, 1962.
Buchanan, J.M. and Tullock, G., *Calculus of Consent*, Ann Arbor, Michigan 1962.
Buchanan, J.M., 'The Relevance of Pareto Optimality', *Journal of Conflict Resolution*, vol 6, 1962.
Buchanan, J.M., 'In Defence of Caveat Emptor', *University of Chicago Law Review*, vol 38, Fall 1970.
Buchanan, J.M., 'Positive Economics, Welfare Economics and Political Economy', *Journal of Law and Economics*, vol 2, (pp. 124–38) 1959.
Bull, J.P. and Roberts, B.J., 'Road Accident Statistics – A Comparison of Police and Hospital Information', *Accident Analysis and Prevention*, vol. 5, 1973.
Burrows, P., 'On External Cost and the Visible Arm of the Law', *Oxford Economic Papers*, vol 22, 1970.

Calabresi, G., *The Costs of Accidents*, Yale University Press, New Haven 1970.
Calabresi, G., 'Right Approach, Wrong Implications; A Critique of McKean on Products Liability,' *University of Chicago Law Review*, vol 38, 1970–71.
Coase, R., 'The Problem of Social Cost', *Journal of Law and Economics* vol. 3, 1960.
Codling, P.J., 'Thick Fog and its Effect on Traffic Flow and Accidents', *TRRL Report* LR377, 1971.
Conard, A. F. et al., *Automobile Accident Costs and Payments, Studies in the Economics of Injury Reparation.* Ann Arbor, Michigan, 1964.
Culyer, A.J., *The Economics of Social Policy,* Martin Robertson, London 1973.
Dawson, R.F.F., 'Current Costs of Road Accidents in Great Britain', *TRRL Report LR396,* 1971.
Demsetz, H.H., 'Some Aspects of Property Rights', *Journal of Law and Economics,* vol. 61, 1966.
Demsetz, H.H., 'Information and Efficiency: another viewpoint', *Journal of Law and Economics,* vol. 12, 1969.
Department of the Environment, *Getting the best roads for our money: The COBA method of appraisal,* HMSO, 1972.
Diamond, P.A., 'Accident Law and Resource Allocation', *Bell Journal of Economics and Management Science*, vol 5, no. 2, Autumn 1974.
Dorfman, R., 'The Economics Product Liability. A reaction to McKean', *University of Chicago Law Review,* vol. 38, 1970–71.
Dunn, J.B., 'Traffic Census Results for 1971', *TRRL Report* LR 548, 1973.
Ghosh, D., 'An Analysis of Social Costs from Accidental Personal Injuries', Discussion Paper No. 24 in *Discussion Papers in Industrial Economics,* Department of Industrial Economics, University of Nottingham, April 1975.
Ghosh, D. and Lees, D., 'Changing Patterns of Traffic and Weather Effects on Road Casualties in Great Britain', Discussion Paper No. 1 in *Discussion Papers in Industrial Economics,* Department of Industrial Economics, University of Nottingham, September 1974.
Ghosh, D. and Lees, D., 'Cost and Compensation for Personal Injuries in Industrial Accidents: A Case Study', Discussion Paper No. 18 in *Discussion Papers in Industrial Economics,* Department of Industrial Economics, University of Nottingham, February 1975.
Ghosh, D., Lees, D. and Seal, W., 'Effects of Traffic Flows and Speed on

Motorway Casualties in Great Britain, January 1972 to March 1974', Discussion Paper No. 8 in *Discussion Papers in Industrial Economics*, Department of Industrial Economics, University of Nottingham, October 1974.

Ghosh, D., Lees, D. and Seal, W., 'Death on the Motorway', *New Society*, 22 August 1974.

Ghosh, D., Lees, D. and Seal, W., Optimal Motorway Speed and Some Valuations of Time and Life', *The Manchester School*, June 1975.

Goldberg, V., 'The economics of product safety and imperfect information', *The Bell Journal of Economics and Management Science*, vol. 5, no 2, Autumn 1974.

Harrison, A.J. and Quarmby, D.A., 'The value of time', in *Cost Benefit Analysis*, R. Layard (ed.), Penguin, 1972.

Heineke, J.M., 'A note on modeling the criminal choice problem', *Journal of Economic Theory*, vol. 10, 1975.

Hirschleifer, J., 'Where are we now in the economics of information?', *American Economic Review* (Papers and Proceedings), vol 63, 1973.

Hochman, H.H. and Rodgers, J.D., 'Pareto Optimal Re-distribution', *American Economic Review*, vol. 60, 1970.

Illich, I., *Medical Nemesis: The Expropriation of Health*, Calder & Boyars, London 1975.

Layard, R. (ed), *Cost Benefit Analysis*, Penguin, Harmsworth, 1972.

Lee, N. and Dalvi, M.Q., 'Variations in the Value of Travel Time', *The Manchester School*, September 1969.

Lee, N. and Dalvi, M.Q., 'Variations in the Value of Travel Time: further analysis', *The Manchester School*, September 1971.

Lees, D.S. and Doherty, N., 'Compensation for Personal Injury', *Lloyds Bank Review*, April 1973.

Lees, D.S. and Rice, R.G., 'Uncertainty and the welfare economics of medical care: a comment', *American Economic Review*, vol. LV, no. 1, March 1965.

McKean, R.N., 'Products Liability: Implications of Some Changing Property Rights', *Quarterly Journal of Economics*, vol. 84, 1970.

McKean, R.N., 'Products Liability: Trends and implications', *University of Chicago Law Review*, vol. 38, Fall 1970.

McKean, R.N., 'Property Rights within Government, and Devices to Increase Governmental Efficiency', *Southern Economic Journal*, vol. 39, 1972.

Meade, J.E., *The Theory of Economic Externalities: The Control of the Environmental Pollution and Similar Social Costs*, Sithoff, Leiden 1973.

Millward, R., *Public Expenditure Economics,* McGraw-Hill, London 1971.
Ministry of Transport, *How Fast,* HMSO, 1968.
Mishan, E.J., 'The value of life', *The Journal of Political Economy,* 1971.
Moore, R.L. and Cooper, L., 'Fog and Road Traffic', *TRRL Report* LR 446, 1972.
Munden, J.M., 'An experiment in enforcing the 30 m.p.h. speed limit', *TRRL Report,* LR 24, Harmondsworth, 1966.
Nader, R., *Unsafe at any speed,* Grossman, New York, 1965.
O'Connell, J., *'The Injury Industry and the Remedy of No-fault Insurance'* Illinois U.P., Urbana 1972.
Oi, W.Y., 'The economics of product safety: a rejoinder', *The Bell Journal of Economics and Management Science,* vol. 5, no. 2, Autumn 1974.
Oi, W.Y., 'The Economics of Product Safety,' *The Bell Journal of Economics and Management Science,* vol. 4, no. 1, Spring 1973.
Oi, W.Y., 'On the economics of industrial safety', *Working Paper 48, Industrial Relations Section,* Princeton University, June 1974.
Palda, K.S., *The Measurement of Cumulative Advertising Effects.* Prentice-Hall 1972.
Pauly, M.V., *Medical Care at Public Expense,* Praeger, New York, 1971.
Peranio, A. 'Conceptualisation and use of road safety and traffic engineering formulas', *Traffic Quarterly,* 1971.
Pigou, A.C., *The Economics of Welfare,* 4th edition, Macmillan, London, 1932.
Posner, R.A., 'A theory of negligence', *Journal of Legal Studies,* vol. 1, 1972.
Rawls, J., *A Theory of Justice,* Clarendon Press, Oxford, 1972.
Road Accidents in Great Britain, 1972, 1973, HMSO.
Road Research Laboratory, 'Report on the 70 m.p.h. Speed Limit Trial', *RRL Special Report,* no. 6, HMSO, 1967.
Road Research Laboratory, 'Road accidents in December 1964 and January 1965' *Road Research Technical Paper,* no. 79, HMSO, 1965.
Robens, Lord, *Safety and Health at Work,* Report of the Committee 1970–72, HMSO, July 1972.
Schelling, T.C., 'The Life You Save May Be Your Own', in S.B. Chase (ed.) *Problems in Public Expenditure Analysis,* The Brookings Institution, Washington DC, 1968.
Sen, A.K., *Collective Choice and Social Welfare,* Holden-Day, San Francisco, 1970.
Shibata, H., 'A bargaining model of the pure theory of public expenditure', *Journal of Political Economy,* vol. 79, 1971.
Smeed, R.J., 'Some statistical aspects of road safety research', *Journal of*

the Royal Statistical Society, Series A 112, 1949.

Smeed, R.J., 'The usefulness of formulae in traffic engineering and road safety', *Accident Analysis and Prevention*, vol. 14, 1972.

Solow, R.M., 'Technical change and the aggregate production function', *The Review of Economics and Statistics*, vol. XXXIX, 1957.

Steele, G.R., 'Industrial accidents: an economic interpretation', *Applied Economics*, vol. 6, 1974.

Street, H., *The Law of Torts*, 5th edition, Butterworth, London 1972.

Tullock, G., 'The charity of the uncharitable', *Western Economic Journal*, vol. 8, 1970.

Tullock, G., *The Logic of the Law,* Basic Books, New York, 1971.

Turvey, R., 'On divergences between social cost and private cost', *Economica,* vol. XXX, 1963.

Williamson, O.E., Olson, D.G., and Ralston, A., 'Externalities, insurance and disability analysis', *Economica*, August 1967.

Woodhouse Report, *Royal Commission to Inquire into and Report upon Workers' Compensation,* Owen, Wellington, 1967.

Wright, C.C., 'A new technique for estimating motorway speeds and some results obtained under the emergency 50 m.p.h. limit', *Institute of Highway Engineers,* October 1974.

Index

Some index references are to footnote indices. If a subject cannot be found on the page quoted, reference to the notes at the end of the chapter will provide a lead.

Accident externalities 43-9, 106-11
Accident occurrence, economic theory of 56
Accidents:
   can they be eliminated? 39-40
   comment on definition of 1
   economic consequences of 1-2
   involving driver only 87
   (non-traffic) and medical aspects 87-8
   other than traffic 87-100:
      classification 87-9; product liability 89-92; industrial 92-5, 97-100; statistics of 95-7
   research into *see* Research
   the law on 49-50
   see also Road accidents
Ackroyd and Bettison (1974) 30
Administrative costs and compensation 114
Advertising, effects of 9
Alessi (1968) 107
Arrow (1963) 104-5; (1965) 111; (1971) 112-13
Atiyah (1970) 114

Becker (1965) 77; (1968) 55, 60-1
Bernoulli (1954) 103
Birmingham Accident Hospital 22
Brown, J.P. (1973) 44, 55
Buchanan (1959) 111; (1962) 50, 54, 102; (1969) 42-3, 90-2
Buchanan and Stubblebine (1962) 43, 44, 106
Buchanan and Tullock (1962) 48
Bull and Roberts (1973) 22, 79
Burrows (1972) 44-5

Calabresi (1970) 2, 41, 43, 54-6, 91-2, 102, 110, 113-14
Case study: in quantum damages 114-24; method of research into 6
Caveat emptor and vendor rule 89

Civil litigation *see* Tort
Classification of non-traffic accidents 87-9
Clean Air Act, 1956 31
Coase (1960) 44, 102
Cobb-Douglas 20
Codling (1971) 31
Compensation:
   economics of 101-24:
      as a social problem 101-13; loss-spreading equity or efficiency 102-3; and insurance 103-6; and post-accident externalities 106-11; and institutional reform 111-13
   compensating schemes, costs of 113-24
   quantum damages, a case of 114-24
   conclusion 124-5
   for injuries 40-1, 87
Conclusions (of this study) 127-8
Conrad et al. (1964) 113
Consumer Product Safety Commission (US) 88
Cost benefit variables 76-7, 93
Costs of compensating systems 113-24
Culyer (1973) 84

Damages at Common Law 94: quantum of (a case study in) 114-24
Darkness and accidents 21
Dawson (1971) 78
Demsetz (1966) 53, 111
Department of Environment (HMSO - 1972) 68, 79
Diamond (1974) 56
Disablement, allowances for and value of 101, 107, 125
Dorfman (1970-71) 91-2
Drinking and driving 7, 9, 12
Driver only accidents 87
Durbin-Watson Statistic 124

135

Economics and 'new' law 54-6
Efficiency and loss-spreading in compensation 102-3
Employers' Liability (Compulsory Insurance) Act, 1969 94
Epidemiology: accidents involving 87-8; method of research 5
Equity and loss-spreading in compensation 102-3
Ethical issues 41-3
Experiments 5-6
Externalities and accidents 43-9, 106-11

Factory Acts, reportable accidents under 96
Fatalities, model for 25-8: Smeed's equation for 16
Fog, effects of 31
'Free lunches' 106

Ghosh (1975) 56
Ghosh and Lees (1974) 27; (1975) 115
Ghosh et al. (1974) 28; (1975) 68
Goldberg (1974) 52-3, 90

Harrison and Quarmby (1972) 77, 85
Health legislation, cases escaping 93
Hirschleifer (1973) 52
Hochman and Rodgers (1970) 107-8, 110
Hospitals, obtaining data from 88
How Fast (HMSO - 1968) 25

Ignorance and economics of information 51-4, 102
Illich (1975) 88
Industrial accidents 92-5, 97-100
Industry, groups in 63
Information, costs of obtaining 51-4
Injuries: serious, model for 25-8; slight, limitation of data on 22
Injury Industry, The (O'Connell) 65
Institutional reform and loss-spreading in compensation 111-13
Insurance and loss-spreading in compensation 103-6
Isolation, paradox of 46

Journey time 10
Justice, formal and substantive 49-51

Laboratory tests 5
Lee and Dalvi (1969) 77, 85; (1971) 77, 85
Lees and Doherty (1973) 113-14
Liability insurance 94
Litigation *see* Torts
Loss-spreading *see under* Compensation for injuries, economics of

McKean (1970) 54, 90-1, 102, 110; (1972) 112
Meade (1973) 43
Methodological issues 41-3
Millward (1971) 77
Mishan (1971) 76, 84-5
Model(s): aggregator analysis of road accidents 17-36; and social policy 57-61; and speed 68-75; application of 78-82; for fatalities 25-8; for serious injuries 25-8
Moore and Cooper (1972) 31
Motorways, results of model for 28-36
MOT tests 17
Munden (1966) 5-6

Nader (1965) 89
National Electronic Injury Surveillance System (NEISS) 88
Negligence, concept of 40, 110
'New' Law and economics 54-6

Objectives in social policy *see* Social policy, objectives for
O'Connell (1972) 40, 57, 65, 114, 117
Oi (1973) 90; (1974) 53, 90, 97-9
Optimal speed *see* Speed, what is optimal?

Palda (1972) 9
Paretian approach 42, 54, 92, 101-2
Pauly (1971) 103, 112
Pearson Enquiry 115, 126
Peranio (1971) 16
Petrol, variations in price of 77-8
Pigou (1932) 44
Posner, Professor A.R. 45, 54, 65, 110-11
Product liability (in a non-traffic accident) 89
Public goods, theory of 43-9

Quantum of damages, a case study in 114-24

Rawls (1972) 50
Reform and loss-spreading in

compensation 111–13
Research into accidents 5–13: taxonomy 5–6; application 6–13
Road accidents:
  aggregator analysis of 15–36: introduction 15–17; model 17–22; results of model for all roads 22–8; results for motorways 28–36
  causes of 15–17
Road Accidents in Great Britain (HMSO – 1972) 9
Road Research Laboratory (1965) 8–10, 15, 21; (1967) 9, 15, 21
Road Safety Act, 1967 8–9
Roads, condition of 8, 21
Robens, Lord, Committee of (1970–72) 93–6

Safety legislation, cases escaping 93
Schelling (1968) 84
Seat belts 10, 13
Semi-controlled experiments 5–6
Sen (1970) 42, 50
Shadow prices 82–5
Shibata (1971) 47
Smeed (1949) 16, 26; (1972) 2, 6, 16, 26, 36
Social policy, moving towards 39–63: ethical and methodological issues 41–3; market failure 43–9; accident externalities 43–9; theory of public goods 43–9; formal and substantive justice 49–51; ignorance, uncertainty and economics of information 51–4;
'new' law and economics 54–6; accident occurrence, economic theory of 56; model 57–61; empirical test 61–3
Solow (1957) 17, 19
Speed:
  influence of, as a variable 29
  limits 9
  what is optimal? 67–85: theoretical background 67–8; model 68–75; valuation problem 76–7; application of model 78–82; shadow prices 82–5
Statistical information on non-traffic accidents 95–7
Statistical model building of research 6
Steele (1974) 99

Time, value of 76–7
Torts 40, 44–5, 50, 110, 113
Traffic volume as a variable 29
Transport and Road Research Laboratory valuations (TRRL) 79, 83; *see also* Road Research Laboratory
Tullock (1970) 40, 107; (1971) 51
Turvey (1963) 44

Uncertainty, role of 52, 102

Valuation problem 76–7

Weather elements 21, 23, 29
Williamson et al. (1967) 44
Woodhouse Report (NZ – 1967) 114–24

The Authors

Debapriya Ghosh lectured in India for four years before taking up research at Essex and, later, Sheffield University. He then lectured at the City of Birmingham Polytechnic and is now Senior Research Fellow in the Department of Industrial Economics at Nottingham University.

Dennis Lees was Lecturer and Reader in Economics at Keele University from 1951 to 1965. He then became Professor of Applied Economics at University College, Swansea, before being appointed Professor of Industrial Economics at the University of Nottingham, his present position. He has been Visiting Professor at the Universities of Chicago, California and Sydney.

William Seal worked for two Trust Companies after graduating from Reading University and then took his D.Phil. at York University. He was a Research Fellow in the Department of Industrial Economics at Nottingham University until 1975, when he moved to his present position as Lecturer in Economics at the University of Bath.

Other SAXON HOUSE Studies

Hopwood, A. G.	*An accounting system and managerial behaviour*
Black, I. G., et al	*Advanced urban transport*
Pollock, N. C.	*Animals, environment and man in Africa*
McLean, A. T.	*Business and accounting in Europe*
Rogers, S. J., B. H. Davey	*The common agricultural policy and Britain*
Hermet, G.	*The communists in Spain*
Klingen, J. S.	*Company strategy*
Chrzanowski, I.	*Concentration and centralisation of capital in shipping*
Bailey, R. V., J. Young (eds)	*Contemporary social problems in Britain*
Mack, J. A.	*The crime industry*
Sjølund, A.	*Daycare institutions and children's development*
Lewis, C.	*Demand analysis and inventory control*
Jambrek, P.	*Development and social change in Yugoslavia*
Macmillan, J.	*Deviant drivers*
Richards, M. G., M. E. Ben-Akiva	*A disaggregate travel demand model*
Teff, H.	*Drugs, society and the law*
Snickers, F. et al (eds)	*Dynamic allocation of urban space*
Ellison, A. P., E. M. Stafford	*The dynamics of the civil aviation industry*
Birnbaum, K. E.	*East and West Germany*
Masnata, A.	*East-West economic co-operation*
Ghosh, D.	*The economics of building societies*
Richardson, H. W.	*The economics of urban size*
Starkie, D. N., D. M. Johnson	*The economic value of peace and quiet*
John, I. G. (ed.)	*EEC policy towards Eastern Europe*
More, W. S. (ed.)	*Emotions and adult learning*
Grassman, S.	*Exchange reserves and the financial structure of foreign trade*
Thompson, M. S.	*Evaluation for decision in social programmes*
von Geusau, F.A.M.A. (ed.)	*The external relations of the European Community*
Bergmann, T.	*Farm policies in socialist countries*
Ash, J. C. K., D. J. Smyth	*Forecasting the U.K. economy*
Blank, S.	*Government and industry in Britain*
Buttler, F. A.	*Growth pole theory and economic development*
Richardson, H. W., et al	*Housing and urban spatial structure*
van Duijn, J. J.	*An interregional model of economic fluctuations*
Brittain, J. M., S. A. Roberts (eds)	*Inventory of information resources in the social sciences*
Fukuda, H.	*Japan and world trade*
Jackson, M. P.	*Labour relations on the docks*
Stephenson, I. S.	*The law relating to agriculture*
Hess, H.	*Mafia and Mafiosi*
Vodopivec, K.	*Maladjusted youth*
Hovell, P. J., et al	*The management of urban public transport*
Funnell, B. M., R. D. Hey (eds)	*The management of water resources in England and Wales*
Martin, M. J. C.	*Management science and urban problems*
Rhenman, E.	*Managing the community hospital*
Giddings, P. J.	*Marketing boards and ministers*
Klaassen, L. H., P. Drewe	*Migration policy in Europe*
Chapman, C. B.	*Modular decision analysis*

Hodges, M.	*Multinational corporations and national governments*
Liggins, D.	*National economic planning in France*
Friedly, P. H.	*National policy responses to urban growth*
Madelin, H.	*Oil and politics*
Tilford, R. (ed.)	*The Ostpolitik and political change in Germany*
Friedrichs, J., H. Ludtke	*Participant observation*
Fitzmaurice, J.	*The party groups in the European parliament*
Brown, J., G. Howes (eds)	*The police and the community*
Lang, R. W.	*The politics of drugs*
Denton, F. T., B. G. Spencer	*Population and the economy*
Dickinson, J. P. (ed.)	*Portfolio analysis*
Wilson, D. J.	*Power and party bureaucracy in Britain*
Wabe, J. S.	*Problems in manpower forecasting*
Willis, K. G.	*Problems in migration analysis*
Farnsworth, R. A.	*Productivity and law*
Shepherd, R. J.	*Public opinion and European integration*
Richardson, H. W.	*Regional development policy and planning in Spain*
Sant, M. (ed.)	*Regional policy and planning for Europe*
Thorpe, D. (ed.)	*Research into retailing and distribution*
Dickinson, J. P.	*Risk and uncertainty in accounting and finance*
Hey, R. D., T. D. Davies (eds)	*Science, technology and environmental management*
Britton, D. K., B. Hill	*Size and efficiency in farming*
Buchholz, E., et al	*Socialist criminology*
Paterson, W. E.	*The SPD and European integration*
Blohm, H., K. Steinbuch (eds)	*Technological forecasting in practice*
Piepe, A., et al	*Television and the working class*
Goodhardt, G. J., et al	*The television audience*
May, T. C.	*Trade unions and pressure group politics*
Labini, P. S.	*Trade unions, inflation and productivity*
Casadio, G. P.	*Transatlantic trade*
Whitehead, C. M. E.	*The U.K. housing market*
Balfour, C.	*Unions and the law*